A Guide to High School Success for Students with Disabilities

A Guide to High School Success for Students with Disabilities

EDITED BY CYNTHIA ANN BOWMAN
AND PAUL T. JAEGER

Foreword by Chris Crutcher

Greenwood Press
Westport, Connecticut • London

KH

Library of Congress Cataloging-in-Publication Data

A guide to high school success for students with disabilities / edited by Cynthia Ann
  Bowman and Paul T. Jaeger ; foreword by Chris Crutcher.
    p. cm.
  Includes bibliographical references and index.
  ISBN 0–313–32832–3 (alk. paper)
   1. Teenagers with disabilities—Education (Secondary)—United States—Handbooks,
manuals, etc. 2. Academic achievement—United States—Handbooks, manuals, etc. I.
Bowman, Cynthia Ann, 1958– II. Jaeger, Paul T., 1974–
  LC4031.G85   2004
  371.9′0473—dc22   2004053041

British Library Cataloguing in Publication Data is available.

Library of Congress Catalog Card Number: 2004053041
ISBN: 0–313–32832–3

First published in 2004

Greenwood Press, 88 Post Road West, Westport, CT 06881
An imprint of Greenwood Publishing Group, Inc.
www.greenwood.com

Printed in the United States of America

The paper used in this book complies with the
Permanent Paper Standard issued by the National
Information Standards Organization (Z39.48–1984).

10 9 8 7 6 5 4 3 2 1

9/15/05

Dedicated with love and gratitude to my friend, colleague, teacher, and mentor Nancy McCracken who convinced me to share my experiences to help others understand disability and open doors for acceptance and advocacy.

Cindy

Contents

Foreword   *xi*
  Chris Crutcher

Acknowledgments   *xiii*

Introduction   *xv*

Section I.   Historical Background and Legal Rights   **1**

Introduction   1

The Meaning of Inclusion: The Educational Experiences
of One Teacher with a Disability   3
  Pamela K. DeLoach

Kick at the Darkness: Integration, Education, and the
Struggle for Legal Rights for Individuals with Disabilities   7
  Paul T. Jaeger

Section II.   Culture and Society   **23**

Introduction   23

We're Just More Accommodating   25
  Krista with Jessica

Don't Make Fun of My Sister   26
  Michael

My Best Friend Has Cancer   27
  High School Senior

Disability in Culture; Disability as Culture   28
    Paul T. Jaeger

Feature Films: Public Perception of Disability   36
    Rhonda S. Black

Images of Disability in Literature   45
    Cynthia Ann Bowman and Paul T. Jaeger

Section III.   Interactions and Relationships   **57**

Introduction   57

Sight and Insight: My Life in Public School   59
    David W. Hartman

Extracurricular Activities and Students with Disabilities   66
    Cynthia Ann Bowman

Dating Considerations for Adolescents with Disabilities   70
    Phyllis A. Gordon and Molly K. Tschopp

Section IV.   Academic Issues   **83**

Introduction   83

Volunteering to Rediscover Myself   85
    High School Junior

We Carved Pumpkins and Learned from Each Other   86
    Cindy

Experiences of High School Students with Disabilities   87

Moving On: Ideas for You to Make Your Transition to
High School Great!   89
    Allison P. Dickey

Managing Educational Supports: Advice from Students
with Disabilities   98
    Ann I. Nevin with Stephen, Jamie, and Joanie

Curriculum: To Run the Race   108
    Cynthia Ann Bowman

Libraries, Media Centers, Online Resources,
and the Research Process   117
    Tom McNulty

After High School?   132
    Cynthia Ann Bowman

Curriculum and Disability: Pedagogical Considerations
for Teachers   144
  Cynthia Ann Bowman

Section V.   Advocacy for All   **151**

Introduction   151

I Don't Like the Term Disability   153
  Cheryl

An Important Lesson   154
  High School Student

Advocacy, Empowerment, and Inclusion: Equal Educational
Opportunities for All   155
  Paul T. Jaeger and Cynthia Ann Bowman

Appendix I: Suggested Readings Related to Disabilities   *161*

Appendix II: Online Resources for Students with Disabilities   *170*

Index   *173*

About the Editors and Contributors   *179*

Foreword

Kyle Maynard, a wrestler from Collins Hill High School in Suwanee, Georgia, has no arms below the elbows and no legs below the knees. His record for 2004 qualifies him to wrestle for the state championship at 103 pounds. He uses no apparatus other than a motorized wheelchair; no prosthetics, no gizmos. He types more than 50 words a minute. He can lift more than 200 pounds, 20 times. He is drop-dead handsome, and he is headed for college next year and who knows what after that.

Even as you watch Kyle do his magic, you ask yourself, "How is this possible?" I can't tell you definitively how it is possible, but I'm guessing that it *has* to be because of how his loved ones responded to him from the beginning. He seems to be living his life behaving as if everyone else has his same unique body design.

I know two men—I'll call one Bill and the other Devin. Bill is in his middle fifties and Devin in his early thirties. Both experienced traumatic births that resulted in a weakened side of the body, Bill on the right side and Devin on the left. Bill's parents treated him as if he were like every other kid, supported his academic and athletic endeavors, patiently waded through his frustrations, and loved him like every parent should love his or her child. Conversely, Devin's father was disappointed in him from the moment of birth and angry at the universe for the dirty trick it had played, and he focused that anger and derision on Devin. As a result, Devin grew up physically and emotionally crippled; there's no other word for it. Even though his IQ was above average, he barely graduated from high school and struggles to this day simply to make a living. Bill played center linebacker on his college football team—a team that nearly won an NAIA

(National Association of Intercollegiate Athletics) championship—and went on to enjoy an exemplary career as a teacher and coach. Exact same physical challenges, exact opposite results.

The truth is, most people with disabilities operate somewhere between the extremes of this continuum. Some seem to have an inner resolve that takes on challenges; some crumble in the face of those challenges; and most (like the rest of us) do both, depending on the context of the situation. But we are all affected by the way the world responds to us. It's all about perception.

A Guide to High School Success for Students with Disabilities focuses on people who are perceived as "different" standing up for themselves, taking on the challenges of their circumstances, and rising to a level of human dignity that is a birthright.

As kind and compassionate as our leaders sometimes tell us they are and ask us to be, the American culture can be downright mean. If you don't believe me, sit yourself in a wheelchair for a week or put on a blindfold and see how friendly your environment is. People who are physically and mentally challenged have had to fight for the amenities they do have, like ramped curbs and Braille elevator buttons, because it costs money to make our environment friendly to them; and without being forced, Americans seem reluctant to spend that money. But what is worse, we often avoid people who seem different from us because of our own discomfort. People with disabilities need to whack us on our collective heads to bring us to our senses. An able-bodied person preparing to read this book needs to keep two things in mind. There is a boy in Georgia with no arms or legs who can pin your shoulder blades to the ground until you cry "Uncle!" and theoretical physicist Stephen Hawking, who has ALS, is a hell of a lot smarter than you are.

If you are one of those people classified as "disabled," I'd like to issue a challenge. Look the rest of us in the eye and tell the truth about yourself. Do not accept us when we make the mistake of feeling sorry for you or allow ourselves to let our ignorant embarrassment get in the way of knowing you. When we do that, we are the disabled ones and may need you to jar us into reality. There is nothing more valuable than the truth as told by the person who knows it. Never back down.

Chris Crutcher

Acknowledgments

The editors would like to express their sincere gratitude to all of the people who helped *A Guide to High School Success for Students with Disabilities* become a reality. First and foremost, thank you to every writer whose contributions grace these pages. By sharing your expertise and individual experiences, you have made this book a tremendous resource for students with disabilities and also for the people who care about them. Second, thank you to each person who served as a reviewer for a chapter of this text; your academic, professional, and personal insights helped considerably to refine these materials. In addition, we would like to thank our friends, family, and colleagues who encouraged, supported, and, in some cases, cajoled us through the entire process of putting this volume together. Finally, we have to thank the one person without whom this book simply would not exist—Lynn Araujo at Greenwood Press, who approached us with the idea that became *A Guide to High School Success for Students with Disabilities*. Her initial concept and her ongoing initiative have aided us from start to finish. Thank you, one and all.

Introduction

A *Guide to High School Success for Students with Disabilities* is intended, first and foremost, to provide important information and guidance to students with any kind of disability who are in high school or who will begin high school in the near future. Though there are specific concerns associated with each different type of disability, the issues faced by all these students are very similar.

This book deals with a range of issues in high school and all of the accompanying major life events. It offers guidance, support, experience, and encouragement specifically to high school students with disabilities, providing everything from an explanation of legal rights to guidance on effective study strategies. The various chapters discuss academic, social, and cultural issues, offering insight into the internal dilemmas that students with disabilities will face, as well as the external problems they may encounter through dealing with other students, teachers, and general society.

Those who care about students with disabilities and those who educate them will also find this book of great importance. It is designed so that family members and friends of these individuals can use this text to gain understanding of the special challenges that they will encounter. Further, it is intended to be a reference for anyone who works with high school students with disabilities, including teachers, counselors, administrators, and librarians.

While some chapters may be more useful to students and others may be of greater help to parents or teachers, each chapter discusses important information and raises significant issues to consider for students with disabilities and for everyone who cares about them.

Many of the contributors to this book have experienced high school as a student with a disability. Because they have life experiences involving a number of different disabilities, their perspectives represent a range of insights. Most of the authors teach and/or research the issues of disability. They feel very strongly about helping students with disabilities to navigate the potentially difficult high school years, and they have worked to incorporate lessons and stories from their personal experiences into their chapters.

This book addresses the spectrum of challenges that an individual with a disability encounters in high school. The goal of discussing these topics is to help these students successfully complete high school and find an appropriate path into the future, while also learning to deal with the special social circumstances that come with having a disability. The book is divided into sections that discuss certain themes or sets of issues. Each section begins with an overview that explains the importance of the subject matter and offers a brief summary of its chapters.

Section I presents an introduction to the history of disability and how individuals with disabilities have been treated across cultures and time. This examination of historical issues leads to a discussion of the legal rights of students with disabilities. Section II discusses the cultural and social issues that surround disability in modern society. It presents specific examinations of disability in film and literature, as well as a discussion of disability in general culture and particularly in high school. Section III is devoted to the many kinds of interactions and relationships of high school students with disabilities. It discusses a range of subjects, including working with teachers, making friends with other students in and outside of school, participating in extracurricular activities, and even dating. Section IV discusses issues related to academic success, beginning with a chapter describing how to make a smooth transition from middle school to high school. The other chapters in this section talk in detail about becoming a self-advocate, writing papers, planning for life after high school, and using accommodations and learning strategies for success in the classroom, in the library, in studying. The book concludes with Section V, which is devoted to issues of advocacy and empowerment for high school students with disabilities.

Each section begins with at least one personal story, written by someone with experiences related to disability and high school. Adults reflecting on past experiences wrote some of the stories, while others were written by current high school students. Together, these personal stories provide the firsthand perspectives of students with disabilities, parents of students with disabilities, teachers with disabilities, and a student who grew up with two parents with disabilities. In several cases, the authors asked to have their names withheld, but they still felt that their stories needed to be shared; each conveys a different experience of high school and disability.

The range of perspectives is very important because accessibility is an issue for everyone involved in high school—students, parents, teachers, librarians, and administrators.

This is the first book that attempts to comprehensively address this range of issues for high school students with disabilities. We believe that it will be of great assistance to students with disabilities, to their friends and family members, and to the teachers, guidance counselors, librarians, and administrators who work with them. We also hope this book will provide many life lessons that students with disabilities can carry with them to college, to the working world, and into other events in their futures.

Cynthia Ann Bowman and Paul T. Jaeger, January 2004

SECTION I

Historical Background and Legal Rights

INTRODUCTION

The first chapter in this section is a personal account of the educational experiences, both as a student and as a teacher, of a special education teacher who grew up, went to school, and began teaching before the laws protecting the rights of people with disabilities were passed or implemented. The second chapter presents an introduction to the history of disability and how individuals with disabilities have been treated across cultures and time. This examination of historical issues leads to a discussion of the current legal rights of students with disabilities.

A key element of this section is the explanation of the legal rights that federal disability laws have provided to high school students with disabilities, including the right of inclusion in general education classrooms. The rights provided by the Individuals with Disabilities Education Act and other laws, and how those rights are protected, are carefully explained, as they protect every high school student with a disability. Knowing your rights is the best way to make sure that they are not being violated.

Similarly, knowing the history that led to those legal rights is extremely important, as it reveals how we got to where we currently are. Both chapters in this section describe the history of the education of students with disabilities, but each presents a different perspective. The first chapter discusses the history of the past 30 years, based on the experiences of one teacher who lived that history both as a student and a teacher with a disability. The second chapter is an overview of the history from ancient times to the present.

It should be noted that the second chapter in this section is the longest chapter in the book. It is placed in the beginning of the volume because its historical and legal information creates the backdrop that frames the information in all other chapters. Historical events and current legal precedents heavily influence the contemporary social issues related to disability. The legal rights of students discussed in many other chapters are detailed in this early chapter.

We encourage you to refer to this section when you have concerns about equity issues, your rights to education and employment, and the changing attitudes of society.

The Meaning of Inclusion: The Educational Experiences of One Teacher with a Disability

Pamela K. DeLoach

I have cerebral palsy, which affects my speech, my handwriting, and the way I walk. In 1973, I was accepted into the College of Education at a major university. I was so excited that I was going to school to become a teacher for children with special needs. To my surprise, the excitement only lasted a short time; I quickly found out that I was totally different from the other students in the program. To make matters worse, the professors continually discouraged me, ridiculed my speech, and refused to give me any accommodations.

At the end of one semester, I was called to the main office of the College of Education. My parents wanted to come with me or send a lawyer with me, but I refused, having no idea what was about to happen. On an early December morning, I walked into a huge conference room where 12 professors waited. I was informed that they no longer wanted me in the program. They said that they didn't think I was capable of teaching anyone because of my own special needs, and that they wanted me out as soon as possible. One professor said that I would be flunked out of the program if I didn't leave; another advised me that all I was competent to do was change diapers and maybe, if I were lucky, I would be able to work in a group home. Their biggest concern was getting me out of the College of Education because they felt I was an embarrassment to them. I told them that I was going to be a special education teacher, and I was not leaving. I said that they would have to flunk me out in order to get me to leave, which two professors said they would do. Another professor stated that I would not be allowed to attend his class because of my speech.

The third semester brought more problems with the professors. I was continuously put down and told that I would have to improve myself in order to pass the courses, even though I had begun to work with a private speech tutor to improve my speaking abilities. One professor would not allow me extra time because he said that if I could not keep up with the other students, I should not be in his class. I took his class four times; I think he gave up before I did and finally passed me on the fourth time. There was another meeting held at the end of that semester. The Speech Department said that I was ready—they taped me and said that everything was fine with my speech. That was not good enough for the Special Education Department; they wanted something that I could not give them—perfect speech. They finally agreed that I was cleared out of speech upon the decision of the department chair of speech pathology.

As I entered the last term, I applied for my final internship. As I finished my application, I found out that it was blocked because they did not want me in the public schools. I went back to my practicum teacher and asked to be his intern, but he did not have enough experience to enable me to be with him. He did manage to find a special education teacher to take me for a semester, where I worked in a Junior High classroom with students who were "educable mentally handicapped." I passed the internship and received my diploma from the university's College of Education and also my teacher certification, despite the resistance from the education faculty.

I could not find a job when I graduated, so I decided to substitute teach. I substituted all over the county and still could not find a permanent position. I started to think that maybe that professor was right because my first job was in a group home and I was changing diapers. I remember even having problems with the director of the group home, who had been encouraged to hire me by one of his employees who knew me. I was hired as a behavior associate, but within the next week I was employed as a shift supervisor. I stayed at that job for a year and began to work with the students with severe and profound mental impairments. I went shopping with them and took them in the community many times. I always took the students by myself with no other assistance.

After a year at the group home, I went back to looking for a teaching job, but could not find one. I would be called and interviewed and they seemed to like what I said, but for some strange reason, I was never hired. About six months into this situation, it dawned on me that it could be because of my disability. When a new school was opened, I was hired as a full-time substitute for the summertime. I learned that there were two openings for full-time teachers in the fall, and I tried to arrange to be interviewed. The administrator repeatedly assured me that I would be interviewed, but I still did not get one of the jobs. There were two positions that were filled with teachers from out of the county. In my first year out of the group home, I did not find a full-time teaching job. During the middle of September, a private school called me and offered me a position as a paraprofessional under a certified teacher. At the time of my interview, I was told that I would be expected to write her Individualized Education Programs (IEPs) because she did not know how to do that. This did not make me a very happy or professionally satisfied person.

During those next several months I learned a lot, but I was about to have the opportunity of a lifetime. During that time period, the auditors would come 24 hours in advance and select a student at random, expecting all his documentation to be in order when they returned the next day. Not having a certified teacher in that classroom meant the school would lose thousands of dollars. I was called into the head teacher's office and told to gather all the documentation that I could possibly find to say that I was a certified teacher. At this point, I still did not know what was happening. When I returned to school the next morning, I received a check for six months' back pay. I was in the right place at the right time, and that is how I got my first teaching job.

During my time as a classroom teacher, my disability has always been noticeable. Basically, it has increased the time I have had to spend on lesson plans, report cards, and filling out forms like IEPs. I finally started asking for help, but before computers were commonplace, I had to find someone to write for me. I always have made sure it was my work, which meant I spent many hours handwriting IEPs, report cards, and other documents to accommodate the needs of the teacher who was rewriting them for me.

In 1991, I joined the Council for Exceptional Children (CEC). A dear friend of mine talked me into attending a national convention. I never knew such wonderful things were happening for my students, as well as for my profession. I had been teaching for more than 12 years and never knew anything about what was taking place outside of my school or my county. That year I learned a new word—inclusion—and it fascinated me. Soon after, it seemed that the biggest issue for students in the special education centers was that they finally had the right to be educated in the neighborhood schools. I jumped on the opportunity, and began looking for a school where I could work with students with disabilities in a general education environment. At the first interview I went on, the administrator offered me a job, and even told me that if I continued to look, they would hold a position for me for two weeks. This was a wonderful feeling, and I accepted the job. I had a new class, a new school, and, for the first time in my career, I was with general education students and general teachers. I had a wonderful paraprofessional who did all my writing for me. Because I can use a computer, when the county acquired computers for the school and the classroom, I began to complete tasks more quickly.

My disability has never been an issue at this school. I have always had people handwrite things for me, and there are now computers in the classroom. I asked for assistive technology for my students, and I have created computer-generated lesson plans that look just like the ones at school. I use a laptop to keep data for my students and I can even generate report cards from the same program. I use an AlphaSmart to take notes. A few years back, I was at a workshop and someone remarked, "The world has finally caught up with Pam DeLoach."

Kick at the Darkness:
Integration, Education, and
the Struggle for Legal Rights
for Individuals with Disabilities

Paul T. Jaeger

INTRODUCTION: THE IMPORTANCE OF EDUCATION
IN AN INTEGRATED ENVIRONMENT

The United States is popularly perceived as a nation that provides equal opportunity for all. To many Americans, "free public education is often thought of as a hallmark of American society" (Gartner & Lipsky, 1999, p. 100). However, legal rights for individuals with disabilities are very recent developments. As late as the mid-1970s, students with disabilities in the United States did not have the legally guaranteed right to attend public schools. Many other legal rights for people with disabilities were not established until 1990, when the Americans with Disabilities Act (42 U.S.C.A. § 12101 et seq.) became law. The story of this struggle dates back through recorded history, culminating with the recent recognition of equal rights for individuals with disabilities to education, employment, and many other facets of society.

The history of the integration of people with disabilities is an extremely important story with failures and victories, heroes and villains. Many of the early advocates for the rights of individuals with disabilities faced condemnation from society. Yet, like Don Quixote charging into windmills, they tried to do what they thought was right in spite of enormous pressures against them. Their valiant work helped lead to the rights that all individuals with disabilities in the United States now possess, including the right to a free appropriate public education in an integrated environment.

Documents such as the Declaration of Independence and the Constitution state explicitly that the U.S. government was founded on concepts of liberty, freedom, and equality. In practice, however, those ideals were not immediately available for all. Though integration is most commonly associated with equal rights based on racial characteristics, the nation has been in a near-constant process of working toward integration for various groups. Just as *Brown v. Board of Education* (1954) was the landmark case mandating racial integration, *PARC v. Commonwealth of Pennsylvania* (1971), *Mills v. Board of Education* (1972), and *Matthews v. Cherry* (1975) were the landmark legal decisions that firmly established the mandate for the integration of individuals with disabilities into society. Integration, in education and other arenas, is extremely important for individuals with disabilities. The segregation of these individuals "creates harmful myths and stereotypes" and leads to biased attitudes that people with disabilities "do not need inclusion or are not even capable or worthy of it" (Shapiro, 1993, p. 142).

In the United States, federal laws now provide individuals with disabilities the right to receive a free appropriate public education in the most integrated setting possible. "Equal access to, and subsequent success in, education is the gateway to changing many other areas of life for individuals with disabilities" (Jaeger & Bowman, 2002, p. 163). It is vital for people with disabilities to truly understand their legal rights in education. To do this, it is necessary to first recognize the difficult journey to the legal right of integration.

THE LONG, DARK TIME AND THE OCCASIONAL DON QUIXOTE

The history of the treatment of individuals with disabilities is exceptionally bleak. Until recently, the record of disability has been one of social exclusion (Bessis, 1995). The earliest known legal classification of people with disabilities dates to ancient Hebraic law (Stiker, 1999). Societies that based their legal systems on the Old Testament of the Bible also had legal classifications of disability (Daniels, 1997). At the height of civilization in ancient Greece and Rome, what is now considered humankind's classical period, disability was "all but invisible, save a few blind prophets" (Edwards, 1997, p. 29). It was socially acceptable to abandon babies born with disabilities, tied or staked down on sunny hillsides, so as to perish in the sun (Garland, 1995). The law of the Greek State of Sparta, at the apex of its power, actually mandated the killing of children with disabilities, leaving the family no choice in the matter (Stiker, 1999; Garland, 1995). The fate of those who escaped death could be rather unpleasant; for example, Balbous Balaesus the Stutterer, a Roman citizen, was kept in a cage along the Appian Way so travelers could be amused by his speech (Garland, 1995).

The Code of Justinian, compiled beginning in 533 CE under orders of Roman emperor Justinian, created a unified code of civil law for the empire that had a tremendous impact on laws of most of Europe until well into the eighteenth century. This code and companion digests of Roman case law detailed many legal rights that individuals with certain types of disability, particularly those with mental, visual, or hearing impairments, were not allowed to have, such as the right to inherit property (Watson, 1998). The situation really didn't improve much for many centuries, as the mistreatment, abuse, neglect, and abandonment of individuals with disabilities have been commonplace throughout human history. People with disabilities have often provoked "a kind of panic both internal and public" that has resulted in oppression, exclusion, and banishment to wretched institutions in many instances (Stiker, 1999, p. 9).

Even in the supposedly more enlightened periods of human history, individuals with disabilities have still faced unfortunate popular movements that emphasized institutionalization in poorhouses or worse, segregation, eugenics, sterilization, and forced relocation to colonies. During the Reformation (1500–1650), both John Calvin and Martin Luther advocated the belief that people with mental disabilities were created by Satan; while in Renaissance (1300–1500) times, it was common to beat individuals with mental or cognitive disabilities on the head as a "treatment" (Braddock & Parish, 2001). Over time, social perceptions have included viewing individuals with disabilities as evidence of the wrath of a supernatural power (Rosen, 1968), as a prophetic sign of negative future events (Warkany, 1959), as useless things (Stone, 1999), as amusement (Hibbert, 1975), as fodder for public sport (French, 1932), and as sufferers of demonic possession (Bragg, 1997).

During the long, dark period of oppression and exclusion of individuals with disabilities, a few brave and egalitarian souls did recognize the need to educate these people and treat them as human beings. The first attempts at creating a system of education for individuals with disabilities were made primarily by farsighted people who understood that equality should extend to those with disabilities and who were willing to accept the risks that came with that belief.

In North America, the earliest known attempt to educate an individual with a disability occurred in 1679, when a private tutor named Phillip Nelson began trying to teach a deaf child to communicate in a systematic manner (Fay, 1899). The community in which he and the student lived forced Nelson to stop teaching the child because the local church denounced his work as blasphemy for attempting to perform a miracle and threatened Nelson's life (Fay, 1899). This irrational opposition to educating individuals with disabilities was heavily influenced by the Puritan belief that a disability was unquestionably a manifestation of divine punishment (Covey, 1998). The perception of disability as heavenly wrath was popularized by Increase Mather, who was an early president of Harvard University, and his son, Cotton Mather, who is most famous for being a driving force behind the burning of those accused of witchcraft (Covey, 1998; Winship, 1994). In fact, people with disabilities in colonial America were often forced out of communities and sometimes even sent back to Europe (Shapiro, 1993).

About the same time that Phillip Nelson's life was being threatened for educating a deaf child, Jan Amos Komensky was writing and advocating in Eastern Europe about the need to reform education so that it was provided equally to all children, regardless of class, status, or ability (Salder, 1966). Komensky's views were not widely accepted, however, as he faced exile and ridicule in his lifetime (Salder, 1966). Fortunately, the situation began to improve in the 1700s.

A method for teaching communication to deaf individuals developed by a Spanish monk named Pedro Ponce de Leon around 1510 came to be widely recognized in Spain and France by the eighteenth century (Daniels, 1997). Ponce de Leon's early methods of teaching sign language inspired a number of European educators and reformers to create residential schools for the deaf, and later the blind, offering the first systematized education for individuals with disabilities (Winzer, 1997). In 1752, Benjamin Franklin and a physician named Thomas Bond founded the first general hospital in colonial America offering care and rehabilitation for individuals with disabilities (Morton, 1897). In the late 1700s and early 1800s, many European nations began to offer private, and sometimes even public, education to children with a wide range of disabilities (Winzer, 1993). Jean-Marc-Gaspard Itard gained international attention at the turn of the nineteenth century for his successful efforts to educate a boy with cognitive disabilities who had been abandoned by his family. Itard taught the child, who was publicly known as the "wild boy of Aveyron," to communicate in speech and sign, to function in social situations, and to perform many skills. Itard's carefully documented efforts laid the foundation for many modern special education techniques (Smith, 2001). In 1829, Louis Braille introduced the embossed dot code, through which individuals with visual impairments could read text in a tactile manner, a method that would evolve into Standard English Braille.

In the United States, the first private education for students with visual impairments was offered in 1812, and private schooling for people with hearing impairments first began in 1817 (Shapiro, 1993). In the 1840s, the first treatise of education of individuals with disabilities was published in the United States (Seguin, 1846). Inventor and social advocate Alexander Graham Bell, whose creations include the telephone, worked to popularize special education in the United States, as well as the use of the term "special education" (Winzer, 1993). In the 1880s, Helen Keller gave disability a publicly identifiable face through her childhood accomplishments of learning to read, write, and speak despite being blind and deaf and not having the benefit of a trained special educator. After graduating from Radcliffe in 1904, Keller became an advocate for the rights of women, racial minorities, the poor, and individuals with disabilities (Loewen, 1995). In 1905, the first special education training courses for teachers were offered in the United States (Smith, 2001).

These advances, however, were occurring in a climate where more powerful social forces still worked to oppress, marginalize, and eliminate individuals with disabilities. Sir Francis Galton, a cousin of Charles Darwin and a scholar who launched the science of modern meteorology, popularized a movement known as eugenics, which was based on the principle that only certain people had the right to have children. In a series of popular books, such as 1869's *Hereditary Genius: An Inquiry into Its Laws and Consequences*, Galton wrote of the need to eliminate undesirable elements, thus raising the standards of humankind. His biased and unscientific theories became popular in the late nineteenth and early twentieth centuries in the United States, leading to many disturbing proposals by legislators and other policymakers. Some of these horrifying ideas included placing all individuals with disabilities on islands by themselves, isolating them by gender, permanently locking them in institutions, or segregating them from the rest of society in a secluded part of a sparsely populated state.

The theory of eugenics, combined with other biases against individuals with disabilities created some truly horrifying consequences. In 1914, the University of Washington and a self-proclaimed Foundation for Child Welfare conducted a study of the laws of the 49 states, territories, and the District of Columbia related to individuals with disabilities (Smith, Wilkinson & Wagoner, 1914). The results are a parade of discrimination, brutal oppression, and dehumanization, though the authors make no comments about the nature of the laws, demonstrating their social and cultural approval. Of the 49 states, territories, and the District of Columbia, 38 had laws prohibiting marriage for individuals with disabilities, either completely or until the woman was past the age of reproduction, a violation of which would result in imprisonment in many cases. Twelve of the states actually had detailed laws prescribing the "asexualization" of people with many types of disabilities (Smith, Wilkinson & Wagoner, 1914, pp. 16–33). Most states had laws mandating the institutionalization of individuals with various physical, mental, and cognitive disabilities. Alabama, Connecticut, Illinois, Indiana, Missouri, New York, Texas, and Virginia even passed laws establishing euphemistically named "colonies" or "villages" where people with certain conditions could be sequestered from the rest of society.

In the early 1920s, a motion picture entitled *The Black Stork* was made to laud the real-life crusade of one doctor who thought that children with disabilities, who are called "defectives" throughout the film, should be "treated" with euthanasia rather than medical attention (Pernick, 1997, p. 92). From 1922 to 1937, the U.S. Public Health Service released

The Science of Life, a set of 12 filmstrips for use in high school biology classes that equated disability to many forms of death and ugliness, including dying cattle, and promoted the notion of the sterilization of individuals with disabilities (Pernick, 1997). The U.S. Supreme Court upheld the legality of these laws so that the United States would not be "swamped with incompetence" and to "prevent those who are manifestly unfit from continuing their kind" (*Buck v. Bell*, 1927, p. 207). The eugenics-based sterilization laws of California actually became the model for the laws passed in Nazi Germany that led to the sterilization of between 300,000 and 400,000 people and the subsequent murder by euthanasia of at least 200,000 individuals with disabilities (Reilly, 1991). Other nations that passed eugenics laws included the United Kingdom, Australia, and many nations of continental Europe (Baker, 2002). When Britain passed laws similar to those of California, the prestigious scientific journal *Science* ran an editorial in 1933 lauding these efforts, advocating the sterilization of those with any mental impairment, many emotional illnesses, visual or auditory impairments, and various bodily malformations (Davis, 1997; MacKenzie, 1981). The legacy of eugenics laws can still be felt in the laws of many other nations around the world (Garton, 2000; Lowe, 2000).

In this climate of oppression, a few more forward-thinking states began progressive programs of education for individuals with disabilities. Kentucky established the first state school for the deaf in 1823; Boston instituted the first day school for deaf students in 1869 (Weintraub & Ballard, 1982). Certification programs for special education were first created in Minnesota in 1915 and the first cooperative agreements between school districts for provision of special education were created in Pennsylvania in 1919 (Weintraub & Ballard, 1982). In spite of these gains, however, significant progress was very slow in coming. Only approximately 12 percent of children with disabilities in the United States were receiving an education in 1948 (Ballard, Ramirez & Weintraub, 1982). A 1969 study found that only seven states were educating more than 51 percent of children with disabilities (Zettel & Ballard, 1982). Prior to the passage of disability rights laws in the 1970s, education of individuals with disabilities depended on the "generosity of private charity and the largess of state and local governments" and those few disabled children who were allowed into the public schools faced "widespread neglect and abuse from schools" and "isolation and minimal services" (Tweedie, 1983, p. 49).

Before the passage of the first major disability rights laws a little more than three decades ago, the battle for the education and integration of individuals with disabilities was waged primarily by isolated advocates for equality, who, like Don Quixote, tried repeatedly to tackle a seemingly insurmountable obstacle. These heroes include monks, educators, inventors, and a signer of the Declaration of Independence. Their efforts and successes paved the way for the disability rights movement and the ultimate achievement of the legal right to integration and education for individuals with disabilities.

KICK AT THE DARKNESS: THE DISABILITY RIGHTS PROTESTS

After countless years of facing exclusion, segregation, oppression, and worse, individuals with disabilities began to make real, measurable progress toward equality. Inspired by the protest movements of the 1960s, people with disabilities became very active in battling for legal rights in the early 1970s. A series of lawsuits, new national laws, and protests cemented their legal rights to be an equal part of American society.

In 1971, a case held that students with disabilities had a constitutional right to receive a public education. In *Pennsylvania Association for Retarded Children (PARC) v. Commonwealth of Pennsylvania* (1971), a federal district court held that the exclusion of children with disabilities from public schools was unconstitutional. Since the state had endeavored to provide a free public education to all its children, Pennsylvania could not deny access to students with disabilities. The groundbreaking *PARC* case immediately inspired disability rights groups in 36 other states to file suits against their state governments (Spring, 1993). Students with disabilities gained more specific federal rights to public education with the decision in *Mills v. Board of Education* (1972), which invalidated the District of Columbia's policy of excluding these children from attending public schools. The court held that this policy, which had resulted in more than 18,000 students with disabilities not receiving a public education, was a clear violation of the students' rights. The court established the mandate that all students with disabilities deserve a public education, harshly dismissing the school district's claims that it did not have enough funding to educate these students. The court further established detailed due process rights for students with disabilities and gave parents a right of notice and appeal for hearings and decisions regarding the education of their child. The holding in this case provided the basic framework for most state and federal legislation for protecting the interests of students with disabilities.

After these important successes in the courts, the federal government passed the first law to grant specific legal rights to individuals with disabilities—Section 504 of the Rehabilitation Act (29 U.S.C.A. § 701 et seq.). This was different from any previous laws that addressed disability, as it established "full social participation as a civil right" and represented a "transformation" of the legal rights of individuals with disabilities (Scotch, 2001, p. 3). In 1973, President Nixon signed the Rehabilitation Act into law; his administration then promptly did absolutely nothing to implement or enforce it. When Gerald Ford became president, he followed Nixon's lead, and also took no actions that would in any way cause the law to have practical value. For the act to be effective, regulations and guidelines regarding requirements and enforcement had to be created by the Department of Health, Education, and Welfare, whose secretary, David Matthews, simply refused to take the necessary actions. After Section 504 was passed, legal journals were actually still publishing articles that legitimately spoke of a lack of federal government protections for students with disabilities to receive even a minimal education (Stick, 1976; Handel, 1975; McClung, 1974). It took a 1976 lawsuit against the government to force the creation of rules and guidelines for Section 504 (*Cherry v. Matthews*, 1976). In the *Cherry* opinion, the court noted in a perturbed tone that Section 504 was not likely to implement or enforce itself. Even this court order, however, did not get the Ford administration to start work on guidelines for enacting and enforcing Section 504. On the day the court order was issued, Matthews immediately tried to send the matter back to Congress (Fleischer & Zames, 2001), but it was left for the Carter administration, whose officials—primarily the new secretary of Health, Education, and Welfare, Joseph Califano—continued to avoid the issue after taking office. These further delays spurred a festive series of protests by disability rights activists, including wheelchair blockades of certain government offices and the driveway of Joseph Califano's home.

These protests were a tremendous step forward for individuals with disabilities, demonstrating that they finally had hope the situation could be improved. "It is a tremendously tragic commentary upon the United States of America that it was only in 1977 that disabled people came to have enough hope to protest. It took two hundred years—two hundred years—for these people to begin to have hope" (Bowe, 1979, pp. 88–89). The protest in the San Francisco office of Health, Education, and Welfare lasted the longest, during which 60 individuals with numerous types of disabilities stayed 25 days, leaving only after the Section 504 regulations had been signed (Shapiro, 1993). Many of the individuals were actually risking their health or their lives by protesting. During the demonstration, encouragement, food, and supplies came from sources as divergent as McDonald's restaurants, the California Department of Health Services, Safeway markets, a number of labor unions, the Black Panthers, and San Francisco mayor George Moscone (Fleischer & Zames, 2001; Shapiro, 1993). The events that occurred during the demonstrations emphasized the bias these people were fighting against. Califano reportedly ordered that the demonstrators should receive no food and not be allowed communication outside the offices, and the Health, Education, and Welfare officials treated the demonstrators as misbehaving children, offering punch and cookies as a bribe to leave (Shapiro, 1993; Heumann, 1979). The demonstrators in New York faced even more ridiculous and demeaning treatment, including having a registered nurse stay with them to make sure they could look after themselves (Fleischer & Zames, 2001).

The first guidelines for Section 504 finally were signed on April 28, 1977, and formally issued on May 4, 1977, several years after President Nixon had originally signed the law. It took four years of legal maneuvering and political action, culminating in the first major disability rights protests in the United States, to get Section 504 implemented, a job the government should have done immediately without encouragement. However, the demonstrations showed that people with disabilities were willing to do whatever was necessary to gain equal standing in society.

FAPE = INTEGRATION: THE LEGAL RIGHT
TO EDUCATION FOR INDIVIDUALS WITH DISABILITIES

Shortly after the Rehabilitation Act was passed, the Individuals with Disabilities Education Act (IDEA) became the first national law to protect the rights of students with disabilities. IDEA was first passed in 1975 as the Education for All Handicapped Children Act (EAHCA), which established the standard of a "free appropriate public education" for students with disabilities (20 U.S.C.A. § 1400 et seq.). IDEA delineates and codifies many specific rights and protections for these students in public schools. It guarantees that all students with disabilities have the legal right to receive an education in a public school that meets the individual needs of the student in as integrated a setting as possible.

IDEA protects students who have a range of disabilities, including those with cognitive impairments, hearing impairments including deafness, speech or language impairments, visual impairments including blindness, serious emotional disturbance, orthopedic impairments, autism, traumatic brain injury, other health impairments, or specific learning disabilities. IDEA applies to many public school students; annually, approximately 10 percent of students attending public school are protected by IDEA (Hallenbeck & Kauffman, 1994). Usually, more than five million children with disabilities are receiving some form of special education at any time (Vanderwood, McGrew & Ysseldyke, 1998). Since its passage and implementation, IDEA has continued to facilitate the social integration of equality for individuals with disabilities.

IDEA was based on extensive congressional findings that emphasized the need for further improvement in the education of students with disabilities. The act prioritizes educating these students in as typical a situation as possible by integrating them in general education classrooms to the maximum extent feasible. IDEA compels schools to place students with disabilities in the least restrictive environment possible and to integrate them into classes with students without disabilities as frequently as possible. The school that the student with a disability attends is required to be as close to his or her home as available and appropriate. IDEA also provided for more parental involvement in the placement and education of the student. Rather than simply being informed of the school's decision regarding the education of their child, parents were given a greater right to participate in these decisions. IDEA also added due process requirements and appeal procedures to protect the rights of students with disabilities.

Under IDEA, each student with a disability is guaranteed a free appropriate public education (FAPE). An FAPE encompasses the special education, related services, and requirements of the individualized education plan of the student with a disability. According to IDEA, an FAPE is defined as special education and related services that:

Have been provided at public expense, under public supervision and direction, and without charge, meet the standards of the State educational agency, include an appropriate preschool, elementary, or secondary school education in the State involved, and are provided in conformity with the individualized education program. (20 U.S.C.A. § 1401(8))

The meaning of free public education is clear; public schools cannot charge for the education of a student with a disability. Each student with a disability has an affirmative right to be educated in a public school at no cost, just as every other student does.

According to IDEA, special education is "specially designed instruction" which meets "the unique needs of a child with a disability" (20 U.S.C.A. § 1401(25)). Primarily, special education is related to supporting general academic instruction. For some students with disabilities, special education means part- or full-time placement in a classroom environment specifically designed for them. For most students with disabilities, however, special education means receiving some special learning services in a general education classroom, as historically the majority of students with disabilities who receive services are either learning disabled or speech impaired. For a student with a learning disability, the special education might include special testing formats; for visual impairment, the special education would include enlarged print or Braille materials; and for a seriously emotionally disturbed student, the special education could include a specific curriculum to address the emotional issues.

Under IDEA, students with disabilities receive not only the necessary special education, but also the related services needed to support their education. These include, but are certainly not limited to: social work services; assistive technology; physical, occupational, and recreation therapy; audiology; speech pathology; psychological and counseling services; orientation and mobility services; and medical services specifically for diagnostic or evaluative purposes.

IDEA establishes that public schools at the state and local levels would be held accountable for failure to properly educate students with

disabilities. The act provides students and parents with a set of legal enforcement mechanisms to pursue against schools that are not providing
an appropriate education, including relief and compensation for damages.
The right of private suit against the states makes IDEA a significant tool
for improving the education of students with disabilities, as parents are
given a heightened enforcement technique to protect the rights of their
children. If a school system is not providing the appropriate accommodations or is providing none at all, the parents have the ability to sue the
school district in order to assure the free appropriate public education for
students with disabilities, designed to meet the specific needs of each individual student. Under IDEA, an Individualized Education Program (IEP)
has to be created for a student with a disability and reviewed annually.

A student's IEP is the document that details the academic, educational,
and placement needs of that particular individual based on his or her
abilities, as well as the levels at which the student should be performing
and goals that he or she should be accomplishing. It is, in short, the heart
of the application of IDEA. The IEP describes the appropriate course
work, learning environments, and other services for the child, as well as
related academic and educational goals. An IEP can only be developed
following a multidisciplinary evaluation of the student's needs and abilities, including assessment of the nature and extent of the disability.
A school district must use multiple nondiscriminatory tests or evaluations
in the student's native or dominant language. An IEP must be reevaluated
at least once a year.

Created in collaboration between the student's teachers, parents, counselors, and other school personnel, the IEP is a cooperative effort intended to customize the educational process to maximize the learning
potential of the student. Parents are mandatory participants in the IEP
process, with procedural safeguards and appeals in place for disagree-
ments between the parents and school officials regarding the program's
provisions. The IEP must specify the student's current level of performance, his or her measurable educational goals and objectives, and the
special education and related services he or she requires to achieve these
goals. The IEP should detail the starting point and duration of special
programs, the extent to which the student will be integrated into general
education classrooms, and the methods that will be used as a measure of
the student's progress.

Under the requirements of IDEA, a student with a disability must be
placed in the least restrictive environment (LRE) possible that still meets his
or her academic and educational needs. The presumption of LRE is for integration, with segregation of the student with a disability only permitted
when the child cannot be successfully educated in the mainstream classroom. A student with a disability is to be removed from the general educational environment only when "the nature or severity of the disability is

such that education in regular classes with the use of supplementary aids and services cannot be satisfactorily achieved" (34 C.F.R. § 300.550(b)(2)). The LRE for a particular student can be placement in a general classroom for all, part, or none of the day, based on the needs of that individual. The least restrictive environment possible is a general education classroom, while the most restrictive environment possible is a hospital or residential facility. The placement setting has to allow the most time feasible in the general education environment. As an example, for a student with a disability who can perform normally in all classes except mathematics, the LRE would be all general education classes except for the student's math class. If that student were placed in any nonmath special education classes, he or she would not be placed in the least restrictive environment possible.

The concept behind LRE is not to be confused with "mainstreaming" or "inclusion," two educational terms that have become popular without having a formal basis in disability law. Many academics, school officials, and parents have mistakenly taken to using one or both of these terms as synonyms for LRE, though they are not an actual part of the law of IDEA or its regulations. Many educators and scholars currently employ the term inclusion in attempting to describe the LRE requirement of IDEA, speaking of "full inclusion" and "partial inclusion." Despite the potential problems with terminology, the essential concept of LRE is the integration of students with disabilities and other students. LRE ensures that most students with disabilities have the right to be integrated into classrooms with those who do not have disabilities. When students with disabilities are segregated, they suffer from being unable to interact with most other children and become targets of prejudice, discrimination, and pity by many of the other students, as well as many teachers (Hill, 1986). The historical practice of segregating all students with disabilities resulted in their being undereducated, socially stigmatized, and emotionally traumatized (Stick, 1976). For students with disabilities, the psychological benefits of being integrated are enormous. "The biggest benefit will come when students with disabilities feel they 'belong' with the general education children, rather than being segregated in separate classes or separate schools" (Arnold & Dodge, 1994, p. 26).

To protect the rights of a student with a disability, IDEA has a series of substantial safeguards, including parental access to relevant school records; requirement of written notice to parents of proposed changes in their child's educational program; a full, fair, and impartial hearing, with legal counsel if so desired, for educational decisions; the opportunity to appeal any decisions to the courts; the right of the child to remain in current placement while hearings are pending (known as the "stay put" provision); and the ability of the parent to be reimbursed for legal costs and fees if they prevail.

One other important advance of IDEA is that a student with a disability has the right to an education without having to demonstrate that the educational program will be definitively beneficial. IDEA has created a "zero-reject" situation, where every student, regardless of the severity of his or her disability, must be allowed to attend school—students with disabilities cannot be rejected by a public school or denied the opportunity to receive an FAPE. Zero-reject embodies the principle that no student with a disability will again "be subjected to the deplorable state of affairs which existed at the time of the act's passage, in which millions [of students with disabilities] received inadequate education or none at all" (*Timothy W. v. Rochester, New Hampshire, School District*, pp. 960–961).

CONCLUSION

These educational rights for students with disabilities were achieved as a result of the efforts of brave individuals throughout history, from Phillip Nelson to the protestors who occupied the offices of the Department of Health, Education, and Welfare. However, the integration of these students in education has not been greeted with universal approval. IDEA, despite all of the good that it has accomplished, still has its critics, whose arguments display many of the same biases against individuals with disabilities that have been evidenced throughout history. These criticisms, fortunately, can be refuted (Jaeger & Bowman, 2002, pp. 85–96).

As a result of the protections of IDEA, there are now students with disabilities in most general education classrooms. These individuals "continue to forge bridges in all directions: to the nondisabled world, to each other, to the self" (Gill, 2001). A large part of this progress is a direct result of the right to a free appropriate public education in an integrated setting, because "[b]eing educated in an integrated environment increases opportunities for individuals to become fully-functioning, equal members of society" (Jaeger & Bowman, 2002, p. 96). A generation of individuals with disabilities has directly benefited from the legally protected right to a meaningful education in an integrated environment. In order to preserve and extend the significant progress that has been made in the past few decades, people with disabilities must understand their rights, how valuable these rights are, and the sacrifices of those who fought for them.

Throughout the course of human history, the vast majority of individuals with disabilities did not have the right to an equal education; this right, in an integrated setting, may be the most important step toward social equality for these individuals. As the legacy of the previous generations of people with disabilities is the establishment of these rights, the legacy of today's generation will be demonstrating that someone with a disability, when given a fair education, can succeed on absolute terms in education, in the workplace, and in society. Cherish these educational rights, nourish them, and learn everything that you can from your education in an integrated setting. It is the key to personal success and to the future success of all individuals with disabilities.

REFERENCES

Americans with Disabilities Act (ADA), 42 U.S.C.A. § 12101 et seq.

Arnold, J.B. & Dodge, H.W. (1994). Room for all. *The American School Board Journal, 181*(10), 22–26.

Baker, B. (2002). The hunt for disability: The new eugenics and the normalization of school children. *Teachers College Record, 10*(4), 663–703.

Ballard, J., Ramirez, B.A. & Weintraub, F.J. (Eds.). (1982). *Special education in America: Its legal and governmental foundations.* Reston, VA: Council for Exceptional Children.

Bessis, S. (1995). From social exclusion to social cohesion: A policy agenda. Paris: UNESCO.

Bowe, F. (1979). Handicapping America: Barriers to disabled people. In J.P. Hourihan (Ed.), *Disability: Our challenge* (pp. 87–106). New York: Teachers College Press.

Braddock, D.L. & Parish, S.L. (2001). An institutional history of disability. In G.L. Albrecht, K.D. Seelman & M. Bury (Eds.), *Handbook of disability studies* (pp. 11–68). Thousand Oaks, CA: Sage Publications.

Bragg, L. (1997). From the mute god to the lesser god: Disability in medieval Celtic and Old Norse literature. *Disability & Society, 12*, 165–177.

Brown v. Board of Education, 347 U.S. 483 (1954).

Buck v. Bell, 274 U.S. 200 (1927).

Cherry v. Matthews, 419 F. Supp. 922 (D.D.C. 1976).

Covey, H.C. (1998). *Social perceptions of people with disabilities in history.* Springfield, IL: Charles C. Thomas.

Daniels, M. (1997). *Benedictine roots in the development of deaf education: Listening with the heart.* Westport, CT: Bergin & Garvey.

Davis, L.J. (1997). Constructing normalcy: The bell curve, the novel, and the invention of the disabled body in the nineteenth century. In L.J. Davis (Ed.), *The disability studies reader* (pp. 9–29). New York: Routledge.

Edwards, M.L. (1997). Deaf and dumb in ancient Greece. In L. Davis (Ed.), *The disability studies reader* (pp. 29–51). New York: Routledge.

Fay, G.O. (1899). Hartford and the education of the deaf. *American Annals of the Deaf, 44*, 419.

Fleischer, D.Z. & Zames, F. (2001). *The disability rights movement: From charity to confrontation.* Philadelphia: Temple University Press.

French, R.S. (1932). *From Homer to Helen Keller: A social and educational study of the blind.* New York: American Foundation for the Blind.

Galton, F. (1869). *Hereditary genius: An inquiry into its laws and consequences* (1978 ed.). New York: St. Martin's Press.

Garland, R. (1995). *The eye of the beholder: Deformity and disability in the Graeco-Roman world.* Ithaca, NY: Cornell University Press.

Gartner, A. & Lipsky, D.L. (1999). Disability, human rights, and education: The United States. In F. Armstrong & L. Barton (Eds.), *Disability, human rights and education* (pp. 100–118). Philadelphia: Open University Press.

Garton, S. (2000). Writing eugenics: A history of classification practices. In M. Crotty, J. Germov & G. Rodwell (Eds.), *"A race for a place": Eugenics, Darwinism, and social thought and practice in Australia* (pp. 9–18). Newcastle, Australia: The University of Newcastle Press.

Gill, C.J. (2001). Divided understandings: The social experience of disability. In G.L. Albrecht, K.D. Seelman & M. Bury (Eds.), *Handbook of disability studies* (pp. 351–372). Thousand Oaks, CA: Sage Publications.

Hallenbeck, B.A. & Kauffman, J.M. (1994). Integrated special education: United States. In K. Mazurek & M.A. Winzer (Eds.), *Comparative studies in special education* (pp. 403–419). Washington, DC: Gallaudet University Press.

Handel, R.C. (1975). The role of the advocate in securing the handicapped child's right to an effective minimal education. *Ohio State Law Journal, 36,* 349–378.

Heumann, J.E. (1979). Handicap and disability. In J.P. Hourihan, *Disability: Our challenge* (pp. 7–32). New York: Teachers College Press.

Hibbert, C. (1975). *The house of Medici.* New York: William Morrow.

Hill, K.D. (1986). Legal conflicts in special education: How competing paradigms in the Education for All Handicapped Children Act create litigation. *University of Detroit Law Review, 64,* 129–170.

Individuals with Disabilities Education Act (IDEA), 20 U.S.C.A § 1400 et seq.

Jaeger, P.T. & Bowman, C.A. (2002). *Disability matters: Legal and pedagogical issues of disability in education.* Westport, CT: Praeger Publishers.

Loewen, J.W. (1995). *Lies my teacher told: Everything your American history textbook got wrong.* New York: Touchstone.

Lowe, R. (2000). Eugenics, scientific racism and education: Has anything changed over one hundred years? In M. Crotty, J. Germov & G. Rodwell (Eds.), *"A race for a place": Eugenics, Darwinism, and social thought and practice in Australia* (pp. 207–220). Newcastle, Australia: The University of Newcastle Press.

MacKenzie, D.A. (1981). *Statistics in Britain, 1865–1930.* Edinburgh: Edinburgh University Press.

McClung, M. (1974). Do handicapped children have a legal right to a minimally adequate education? *Journal of Law & Education, 3,* 153–173.

Mills v. Board of Education, 348 F. Supp. 866 (D. DC 1972).

Morton, T.G. (1897). *The history of Pennsylvania Hospital 1751–1895.* Philadelphia: Times Publishing House.

Pennsylvania Association for Retarded Children (PARC) v. Commonwealth of Pennsylvania, 334 F. Supp. 1257 (E.D.Pa. 1971).

Pernick, M.S. (1997). Defining the defective: Eugenics, aesthetics, mass culture in early-twentieth century America. In D.T. Mitchell and S.L. Snyder (Eds.), *The body and physical difference: Discourses of disability* (pp. 89–110). Ann Arbor: University of Michigan Press.

The Rehabilitation Act, 29 U.S.C.A. § 701 et seq.

Reilly, P.R. (1991). *The surgical solution: A history of involuntary sterilization in the United States.* Baltimore: Johns Hopkins University Press.

Rosen, G. (1968). *Madness in society: Chapters in the historical sociology of mental illness.* Chicago: University of Chicago Press.

Salder, J.E. (1966). *J.A. Comenius and the concept of universal education.* New York: Barnes & Noble.

Scotch, R.K. (2001). *From good will to civil rights: Transforming federal disability policy* (2nd ed.). Philadelphia: Temple University Press.

Seguin, E. (1846). *The moral treatment, hygiene, and education of idiots and other backward children.* Paris: Balliere.

Shapiro, J.P. (1993). *No pity: People with disabilities forging a new civil rights movement*. New York: Times Books.

Smith, D.D. (2001). *Special education: Teaching in an age of opportunity*. Boston: Allyn & Bacon.

Smith, S., Wilkinson, M.W. & Wagoner, L.C. (1914). *A summary of the laws of the several states governing marriage and divorce of the feebleminded, epileptic and the insane; asexualization; and institutional commitment and discharge of the feebleminded and the epileptic*. Seattle: University of Washington.

Spring, J. (1993). *Conflict of interests: The politics of American education* (2nd ed.). New York: Longman.

Stick, R.S. (1976). The handicapped child has a right to an appropriate education. *Nebraska Law Review, 55*, 637–682.

Stone, E. (1999). Modern slogan, ancient script: Impairment and disability in the Chinese language. In M. Corker & S. French (Eds.), *Disability discourse* (pp. 136–147). Philadelphia: Open University Press.

Striker, H.J. (1999). *A history of disability* (W. Sayers, trans.). Ann Arbor: University of Michigan Press.

Timothy W. v. Rochester, New Hampshire, School District, 875 F.2d 954 (1st Cir. 1989).

Tweedie, J. (1983). The politics of legalization in special education reform. In J.G. Chambers & W.T. Hartman (Eds.), *Special education policies: Their history, implementation, and finance* (pp. 48–73). Philadelphia: Temple University Press.

Vanderwood, M., McGrew, K.S. & Ysseldyke, J.E. (1998). Why we can't say much about students with disabilities during education reform. *Exceptional Children, 64*, 359–370.

Warkany, J. (1959). Congenital malformations in the past. *Journal of Chronic Disabilities, 10*, 84–96.

Watson, A. (Ed.). (1998). *The digest of Justinian*. 2 vols. Philadelphia: University of Pennsylvania Press.

Weintraub, F.J. & Ballard, J. (1982). Introduction: Bridging the decades. In J. Ballard, B.A. Ramirez & F.J. Weintraub (Eds.), *Special education in America: Its legal and governmental foundations*. Reston, VA: Council for Exceptional Children.

Winship, M.P. (1994). Prodigies, Puritanism, and the perils of natural philosophy: The example of Cotton Mather. *The William & Mary Quarterly, 51*, 92–105.

Winzer, M.A. (1993). *The history of special education: From isolation to integration*. Washington, DC: Gallaudet University Press.

———. (1997). Disability and society: Before the eighteenth century. In L.J. Davis (Ed.), *The disability studies reader* (pp. 75–109). New York: Routledge.

Zettel, J.J. & Ballard, J. (1982). The Education for All Handicapped Children Act of 1975 (P.L. 94–142): Its history, origins, and concepts. In J. Ballard, B.A. Ramirez & F.J. Weintraub (Eds.), *Special education in America: Its legal and governmental foundations*. Reston, VA: Council for Exceptional Children.

SECTION II

Culture and Society

INTRODUCTION

This section discusses the cultural and social issues that surround disability in modern society. It presents specific examinations of disability in film and literature, as well as a general discussion of disability in culture and in the high school. It is very important to examine the social issues that surround disability, because they impact how individuals with disabilities are treated in school. These social attitudes, perceptions, and representations influence how other students, teachers, and administrators treat students with disabilities in high school. They also affect how people in positions of power, such as local community leaders, politicians, and school board members, make decisions about the education of students with disabilities.

The stories of individuals who have grown up with disability in their lives begin this section, aptly demonstrating the social and cultural issues that people with disabilities can encounter. The chapter that follows these stories examines disability within the greater social structure. It also examines the culture that these individuals have constructed for themselves with a wide array of similar and shared experiences, creating social connections between all people with disabilities. These connections can also assist students with disabilities to help one another succeed in high school.

The final two chapters in this section detail social perceptions of disability that are revealed in popular media. One chapter examines the portrayal of disability in films and the other in literature. These representations are extremely important to be aware of, as they influence general social perceptions about disability. The manner in which people with disabilities are shown in movies and books has a significant impact on the way they are viewed and treated by others. Understanding the ways in which popular media portray people with disabilities will help these students be aware of the prejudices that may confront them and will provide insight into how to overcome and defeat these prejudices.

We're Just More Accommodating

Krista with Jessica

At first glance, I am a typical teenage girl. I am fourteen years old, have blue eyes, freckles on my face, and curly brown hair. I enjoy playing sports, reading, and I especially love talking. Basically, I talk to anyone who might listen. Even when I go home, my parents listen . . . but they listen differently than everyone else.

From the outside, you cannot see or touch it; it is not written across my face, nor do I carry a sign that tells everyone how truly special I am. However, I am special and I am different. My mom and dad are deaf. Not only does hearing loss affect my mother and father, it affects me as well. As a child, I suffered from severe earaches that caused a slight hearing loss in my left ear. Consequently, I tend to talk in a louder-than-average voice and have to ask my peers to repeat themselves when I cannot read their lips.

Since my parents cannot hear me the way everyone else does, I have learned to communicate with them in various ways. Sometimes I yell or scream, and I also talk with my hands. All of my life, I have spoken to my parents in sign language. At times, the translation between English and sign language leads to miscommunication or confusion.

Besides communicating with my parents through our hands and loud voices, we have other special needs. In order to call my parents on the phone, we use a relay service or TTY [a telecommunications device for the deaf]. Additionally, we watch television by reading the closed caption across the bottom of the screen. I also have had to attend meetings with my parents in order to translate for them.

Although I have been surrounded by disabilities all of my life, I am still a typical teenager. If my peers tell me that my family is not normal, I respond by telling them we are just more accommodating. The adjustments I have had to make in my life have made me more appreciative of the abilities that I have, such as being able to talk to my friends and having parents who are able to listen. I know my parents are special, and I love them for who they are and everything that they have achieved despite the fact that they cannot always hear me.

✍ Don't Make Fun
of My Sister ✍

Michael

My sister was diagnosed with juvenile rheumatoid arthritis when I was just a baby. I remember growing up and learning that she could not do everything I could do. I never noticed her disability until I saw people staring at her and watching her when she was having trouble due to pain. I would have liked to beat them up, but I knew they were focusing on her disability—not the neat person she was. So I learned to stare right back.

I have always been proud of my sister. She is smart, successful, and fun. When I was in high school, she had to have five orthopedic surgeries—on her knees, ankles, and hands. She was in casts all over her body and couldn't move on her own. Before I went to school, I had to help my parents carry her to the bathroom and then to the couch or a wheelchair. As soon as school was over, I would run home and help my mom carry her to the bathroom while my dad was at work. Then I would run back to school for basketball or golf practice. These were two difficult years because my family had to rearrange schedules and work together. Sometimes I would push my sister around the neighborhood in a wheelchair so she could get out of the house. Some people would ignore us, some would smile, some would stop us to talk, and some would say what a good brother I was and ignore my sister. I learned that many people don't understand disabilities, especially physical disabilities. She has so many gifts that people have ignored because of her disability.

I became a pharmaceutical sales representative because I learned how important good doctors and treatment can be. I encourage my own children to look beyond the surface of people to see the wonder and talents of each unique individual. I learned these lessons watching the world watch, and underestimate, my sister.

✍ My Best Friend Has Cancer ✍

High School Senior

In middle school, my best friend went to see her doctor for problems with fatigue, weight loss, and bruising. We thought that she might have mono because many of our friends had gone through similar troubles. After what seemed like forever, she said that something suspicious had been found in her blood and that she needed to go to the hospital immediately. Within days, she was diagnosed with acute myelogenous leukemia and started chemotherapy. She had eight months of treatment in the hospital. We talked on the phone; I went to see her whenever I could find a ride. It was difficult to be in my classes knowing she was in the hospital and also knowing that many of our friends were losing touch with her and didn't know how to act. It was painful for me, as she faced many challenges including intense chemo, many trips to the OR, and an allergic reaction to chemotherapy, a coma, and months of rehab.

I learned that the word cancer scares many people, but I also learned that cancer doesn't always mean that life is over. The fight to rid cancer is an amazingly difficult one, but there is also hope. She has been in remission for five years and we are making plans for college. Having a friend with cancer changed me physically, emotionally, and spiritually. It made me a stronger and more understanding person. It changed how I view life and how I want to spend my life. It taught me about real friendship and the importance of helping others. No one should have to face a difficult situation alone.

Disability in Culture; Disability as Culture

Paul T. Jaeger

DISABILITY IN CULTURE

Many individuals with disabilities have witnessed and experienced significant changes to cultural attitudes about disability in their lifetimes. In the past three decades, as a result of changes in the law, in the attitudes of people with disabilities, and in society, individuals with disabilities have experienced a radical transformation in how they are treated and the ways in which they are able to participate in society. Though discrimination has certainly not been eradicated, and people with disabilities still face serious problems of misunderstanding and discrimination, real progress has been made and continues to occur.

The changes in societal attitudes are reflected by the accepted terms used to describe people with disabilities. The trend has been away from equating the person with his or her impairment to describing the person as happening to have an impairment. Until recently, it was socially acceptable to refer to someone with a disability as a cripple, as handicapped (derived from "cap in hand," a term for begging), or even as defective. The general shift toward using more humane terms to describe the condition of having a disability, such as "individual with a disability," has been fueled by the steps taken by the members of the disability community in asserting their right to be treated as human beings.

The terminology related to particular disabilities has changed mightily as well, also reflecting an emphasis on the person rather than the impairment, which is called person-first language. For example, individuals who use wheelchairs used to be commonly referred to as "wheelchair bound" and people with hearing impairments were called "deaf and dumb." Clearly, both of these terms highlight an inability and make the individual sound close to helpless by using limiting terms like "bound" and "dumb." The terms that are now commonly used for the same conditions, "wheelchair user" and "hearing impaired," acknowledge the disability without implying that the individual is rendered helpless by it. A person may use a wheelchair, but nevertheless can do most anything he or she desires. Someone may have a hearing impairment, but he or she can communicate ideas and express feelings as well as any other person.

Changes in commonly used terms may not seem revolutionary, but they reflect and reinforce slowly evolving attitudes and perceptions of general society toward individuals with disabilities. "To a large extent, disability is a social construct" (Schmetzke, 2002, p. 135). These social constructions can have a profound impact on individuals with disabilities (Gill, 2001); many tend to internalize the social perceptions that they experience (Thomas, 1999). If society uses terms to describe disability that evidence a belief that a person with a disability is unlikely to succeed, then it will be much harder for these individuals to overcome social resistance to their success. If society describes disability in terms that don't reflect a presumption of failure, then someone with a disability is likely to have a better chance of succeeding educationally, professionally, and personally.

The changes in terminology, however, have not served to obliterate the discrimination that individuals with disabilities encounter on a daily basis. In society, disability functions as a "master status," a classification that has more social import to the culture than any other classification in defining the person (Albrecht & Verbugge, 2000, p. 301). The classification of disability "floods all statuses and identities" of an individual, so that "a woman who uses a wheelchair because of multiple sclerosis becomes a disabled mother, handicapped driver, disabled worker, and wheelchair dancer" (Charmaz, 2000, p. 284). In fact, a common bond for all people with disabilities is having to deal with discriminatory cultural attitudes (Jaeger & Bowman, 2002). One individual encapsulated the importance of social classification by noting, "My disability is how people respond to my disability" (Frank, 1988, p. 111). Though the situation has certainly improved greatly in the past few decades, individuals with disabilities still have had many cultural biases to overcome.

One of the most important developments that has allowed people with disabilities to overcome cultural biases has been the institutionalization of their legal rights. The major disability rights laws, such as the Americans with Disabilities Act, the Rehabilitation Act, and the Individuals with Disabilities Education Act, have given these individuals the right to equal treatment in many contexts. Because of these laws, a disability does not limit a person's chance to get an education, go to college and graduate school, and have a meaningful career. At a more basic level, these laws also are intended to ensure that a disability does not prevent a person from entering a building, interacting with the government, or traveling on an airplane. Further, the news coverage of the passage of these laws, especially the Americans with Disabilities Act in 1990, provided many people in society with their first exposure to the concept of disability rights (Fleischer & Zames, 2001). (The story of the creation of these laws and the rights that they guarantee in the context of schools are described in detail in Section I.)

The United States has been the international leader in providing legal rights for individuals with disabilities since Section 504 of the Rehabilitation Act was passed in 1973. People with disabilities have embraced the opportunities created by these laws. For example, individuals with disabilities have proven themselves to be extremely loyal employees to the companies that have given them opportunities; a person with a disability is three times more likely to remain with an employer than a person who does not have a disability (Johnson, 2003). Following the lead of the United States, a number of other nations—including Australia, the United Kingdom, Germany, Austria, Finland, Brazil, South Africa, Malawi, Uganda, and the Philippines—adopted laws or amended their constitutions in the 1990s to provide the first real legal rights for individuals with disabilities (Metts, 2000). However, the nations that have created affirmative legal classifications of disability remain a distinct minority (Albrecht & Verbugge, 2000). "The social exclusion approach ('out of sight, out of mind') is still very prevalent in the world" (Albrecht & Verbugge, 2000, p. 299).

Another major area that has helped individuals with disabilities become integrated into the cultural mainstream has been technology. Advances in information technology in the past 20 years have occurred at astounding speed. Many of these technological innovations, such as computers and the Internet, have made it possible for people with disabilities to accomplish much more than they previously could and to complete many of these things much more efficiently.

My own experiences with a visual impairment provide a decent example of how changes in technology have influenced the way I can perform research. When I first started school (in the 1970s), a personal computer was more myth than reality for most people. I can remember my whole second grade class being taken to a classroom and shown the new school computer in 1981. Yes, there was only one computer, and it was described in hushed and reverential tones. However, for me, the screen was basically unreadable. The type was small and I could barely discern the color of the display, neither of which could be adjusted. I was not impressed.

Flash forward about 10 years and, from my perspective, computers were doing much more interesting and helpful things. The colors on the screen could be changed and the whole screen magnified. I could read the screen without difficulty, since the size of the characters could be enlarged with ease. A few years after that, I got my first optical character reader software. Although the voice sounded distressingly close to Darth Vader with serious sinus problems, my computer could actually tell me what a document said. These types of features, which are so common now, really were revelations when I first got them. Computers were not only useful, they could help me do research and read things that I previously couldn't. Reading information off of a computer screen was easier than reading a book. And the popularization of the Internet, of course, changed things more significantly, as the readable computer screen could now be a portal to an infinite amount of information. None of these possibilities, however, had crossed my mind the first time I saw a computer.

My personal experiences can be multiplied by the number of people there are who have disabilities. The rapid technological changes, especially in the past decade, have dramatically affected how these individuals can participate in society, providing ways for them to contribute more extensively, and generally helping to alter societal perceptions of people with disabilities. A doctor with a hearing impairment, a teacher in a wheelchair, or a lawyer with a visual impairment certainly can change attitudes about what a person with a disability can do. In every case, each person likely benefits from recent advances in technology in his or her career.

The advances in law and technology have undoubtedly altered many cultural perceptions of disability. That does not mean, however, that there are no longer many cultural obstacles for people with disabilities to overcome. The issues that confront these individuals are diverse and multitudinous. There are many critics of the integration of students with disabilities into general education classrooms (Jaeger & Bowman, 2002), and many of the teachers and administrators who work with these students do not have a sufficient understanding of disability (Hahn, 1997). Many ways in which disability is represented (in art, literature, and commercials) continue to reflect the stereotypes that have been used for centuries (Bowman & Jaeger, 2003). In various scholarly fields, the disability is often still equated to the person, resulting in much of the research about disability reflecting bias or being simply offensive (Barton, 1996). Many individuals with disabilities view this research as demonstrating and perpetuating negative social myths and stereotypes (Kitchen, 2000; Stone & Priestly, 1996). Advances in technology have also created new areas where people with disabilities have to work to gain equal rights, such as in access to government information and services that are provided online (Jaeger, in press).

Individuals with disabilities and the cultural perceptions of disability "co-exist within a social reality" (Huber & Gillaspy, 1998, p. 190). The process of changing these perceptions will be an ongoing concern for many years to come. However, a huge amount of progress has been made in the past few decades. One way that people with disabilities can ensure this progress will continue is by working together to understand disability and the cultural roles it plays. Through these types of collaborations over the past few decades, people with disabilities have begun to develop their own culture.

DISABILITY AS CULTURE

At first glance, it may seem odd to talk about a disability culture. Unlike many other attributes that are considered cultures, disability is not necessarily passed from parent to child; in fact, it usually isn't. If you have a disability, your parents, siblings, or children might not, or a close relative may have a different disability. In contrast, other cultural traits, such as race, ethnicity, and religion, are passed from generation to generation. If a child is born to parents of a certain religious faith, it is likely that the child will be raised as a member of that faith. A child born to a parent with a disability, however, is not likely to be raised as though they have a disability if, in fact, they do not. Most cultures have a history that the members celebrate. Individuals with disabilities, on the other hand, have very little to celebrate in their history.

Though there are things that make disability unique as a culture, it still has many cultural attributes. Individuals with disabilities, no matter what their disability is, have shared experiences of struggle, of facing discrimination, and of learning to live somewhat differently than what has been deemed to be normal. The shared experiences of having a disability, any disability, create cultural bonds between these individuals. They often find it easier to discuss their deep feelings about life with a disability when they are talking to other people with disabilities. That comes from the sense of shared experience. I know it is true in my case; the only people I really talk to about how visual impairment makes me feel are other people who have disabilities, even if their disabilities are very different from mine.

People with disabilities are also united by a set of social goals and objectives. As a result of the challenges that they face in society, they are all linked by the goals of being accepted and included by society and being treated with equality and dignity. For individuals with disabilities, true equality "incorporates the premise that all human beings—in spite of their differences—are entitled to be considered and respected as equals and have the right to participate in the social and economic life of society" (Rioux, 1994, pp. 85–86). To work toward this equality, individuals with disabilities have found ways to work together to promote social goals of inclusion and acceptance.

In many cases, they have formed political organizations devoted to promoting civil rights for people with disabilities, from local groups that fight for accessible buses and access to government offices, to national organizations that lobby for legislation (Fleischer & Zames, 2001). Organizations that campaign for civil rights for individuals with disabilities began in earnest in the 1960s (Zola, 1994) and became a national force through protests in the 1970s (Bowe, 1979). In other instances, people with disabilities have created groups that promote their free expression. For example, organizations promoting artistic endeavors for people with disabilities attempt to provide them a "means of self-expression and pride in identity" (Corbett, 1999, p. 171).

Another bond that links these individuals is a set of personality characteristics that are often found in people with disabilities. Having a disability shapes a person's psychological character, being influenced by external events (the way one is treated by other people) and internal events (how a person thinks and feels about him or herself as in terms of a disability). A scholar of psychology and disability has suggested that people with disabilities tend to share certain personality traits:

1. The ability to accept differences between people;
2. The ability to accept human vulnerability and recognize the need to help others;
3. The ability to handle uncertainty and unpredictability;
4. The ability to laugh at disabilities and the problems they cause;
5. The ability to manage multiple tasks simultaneously;
6. An advanced orientation toward future goals and possibilities;
7. A carefully honed capacity for closure in personal communication; and
8. The ability to be flexible, creative, and inspired in situations of limited resources or untraditional modes of operation. (Gill, 1995, pp. 17–18)

Clearly, many of these traits are helpful in dealing with the unique everyday life experiences of a person with a disability. Though not everyone with a disability will possess all of these characteristics, those who read this list usually seem to find a whole lot of themselves in it.

People with disabilities have even begun to develop their own slang terms for concepts unique to the experience of having a disability, such as "crip" and "inspiration station." Crip subverts one of the traditional slurs used against the disabled (i.e., cripple) and turns it around in the same manner that other minority groups have turned hate words into personal affirmatives. This meaning of the term crip has led to the affirmative slogan "Crip is hip," a sign of disability pride and affirmation that has come to adorn T-shirts, bumper stickers, and posters. The term inspiration station refers to a situation in which nondisabled people view a person with a disability as inspiring. This relates to the curious tendency of many members of the general population to claim that an individual with a disability is an inspiration, even if all they are doing is going about their daily activities.

DISABILITY, CULTURE, AND YOU

Though you may not feel a part of the disability culture, it is important to know that it exists and that there are many people with disabilities who have had experiences similar to yours. Living with a disability can sometimes feel very lonely. Even the most upbeat and optimistic person can sometimes feel down as a result of the social challenges that people with disabilities often encounter. When you do have the hard days, don't forget that you are part of a very large community of people around the world who can relate to what you are going through. In fact, about 54 million people in the United States have a disability.

Knowing about the roles of disability in culture and the existence of a disability culture is also important if you want to be culturally active. You can become involved in organizations for people with disabilities, whether social or political. There may be a group for students with disabilities at your school, and there will likely be at least one similar organization in your community. Some groups even exist for people with a particular type of disability, such as hearing or vision impairments. These organizations provide the opportunity to connect with other people with disabilities and to become involved in working to help make life better for everyone in your community.

REFERENCES

Albrecht, G.L. & Verbugge, L.M. (2000). The global emergence of disability. In G.L. Albrecht, R. Fitzpatrick & S.C. Scrimshaw (Eds.), *The handbook of social studies in health and medicine* (pp. 293–307). Thousand Oaks, CA: Sage Publications.

Barton, L. (1996). Sociology and disability: Some emerging issues. In L. Barton (Ed.), *Disability and society: Emerging issues and insights* (pp. 3–17). London: Addison Wesley Longman Ltd.

Bowe, F. (1979). Handicapping America: Barriers to disabled people. In J.P. Hourihan (Ed.), *Disability: Our challenge* (pp. 87–106). New York: Teachers College Press.

Bowman, C.A. & Jaeger, P.T. (2003). *Making diversity more inclusive: Toward a theory of disability based on social, educational, legal, and historical perspectives.* Paper presented at the 2003 American Education Research Association Conference, Chicago.

Charmaz, K. (2000). Experiencing chronic illness. In G.L. Albrecht, R. Fitzpatrick & S.C. Scrimshaw (Eds.), *The handbook of social studies in health and medicine* (pp. 277–292). Thousand Oaks, CA: Sage Publications.

Corbett, J. (1999). Disability arts: Developing survival strategies. In P. Reitsh & S. Reiter (Eds.), *Adults with disabilities: International perspectives in the community* (pp. 171–181). Mahwah, NJ: Lawrence Erlbaum Associates.

Fleischer, D.Z. & Zames, F. (2001). *The disability rights movement: From charity to confrontation.* Philadelphia: Temple University Press.

Frank, G. (1988). Beyond stigma: Visibility and self-empowerment of persons with congenital limb deficiencies. *Journal of Social Issues, 44*, 95–115.

Gill, C.J. (1995). A psychological view of disability culture. *Disabilities Studies Quarterly, 15*(4), 16–19.

———. (2001). Divided understandings: The social experience of disability. In G.L. Albrecht, K.D. Seelman & M. Bury (Eds.), *Handbook of disability studies* (pp. 351–372). Thousand Oaks, CA: Sage Publications.

Hahn, H. (1997). New trends in disability studies: Implications for educational policy. In D.K. Lipsky & A. Gartner (Eds.), *Inclusion and school reform: Transforming America's classrooms* (pp. 315–328). Baltimore: Paul H. Brooks.

Huber, J.T. & Gillaspy, M.L. (1998). Social constructs and disease: Implications for a controlled vocabulary for HIV/AIDS. *Library Trends, 47*(2), 190–208.

Jaeger, P.T. (in press). The social impact of an accessible E-democracy: The importance of disability rights laws in the development of the federal E-government. *Journal of Disability Policy Studies*.

Jaeger, P.T. & Bowman, C.A. (2002). *Disability matters: Legal and pedagogical issues of disability in education*. Westport, CT: Praeger Publishers.

Johnson, A.D. (2003). Americans with Disabilities Act: Is your company compliant? *Diversity Inc.*, June/July, pp. 137–139.

Kitchen, R. (2000). The researched opinions on research: Disabled people and disability research. *Disability & Society, 15*, 25–47.

Metts , R.L. (2000). *Disability issues, trends and recommendations for the World Bank*. New York: World Bank.

Rioux, M.H. (1994). Towards a concept of equality of well-being: Overcoming the social and legal construction of inequality. In M.H. Rioux & M. Bach (Eds.), *Disability is not measles* (pp. 67–108). North York, Ontario: Roeher Institute.

Schmetzke, A. (2002). Accessibility of Web-based information resources for people with disabilities. *Library Hi Tech, 20*(2), 135–136.

Stone, E. & Priestly, M. (1996). Parasites, prawns and partners: Disability research and the role of non-disabled researchers. *British Journal of Sociology, 47*, 699–716.

Thomas, C. (1999). *Female forms: Experiencing and understanding disability*. Buckingham, UK: Open University Press.

Zola, I.K. (1994). Towards inclusion: The role of people with disabilities in policy and research issues in the United States—A historical and political analysis. In M.H. Rioux & M. Bach (Eds.), *Disability is not measles: New research paradigms in disability* (pp. 49–66). North York, Ontario: Roeher Institute.

Feature Films: Public Perception of Disability

Rhonda S. Black

Schools play a very important role in socializing the citizens of a nation. In the United States, they are the primary social institution whereby students learn to be citizens of a democracy. Our society expects schools to teach young people the skills needed for living in this democracy, such as living harmoniously with others and contributing to one's community. However, different people have different ideas about which particular skills are needed and by whom, as well as how these skills should be taught. Schools do not function in isolation; they are heavily influenced by the public's perception of what makes a good society: What should be done and by whom, what skills and abilities are valued, how do people get their opinions about how one should live in society, how do they define success, how do they decide who gets what and how various individuals should be treated? Schools are social institutions and therefore subject to public opinions and the perceptions of the members of society.

As a result, many people influence what happens in schools, including parents, community members, and elected officials. The concepts and ideas of the people affecting the school are shaped, at least partly, by popular images. Therefore, popular films profoundly influence society's perceptions and, consequently, school policies, which in turn influence what we teach, to whom, and where. Stigmatizing media images negatively impact school and societal curricula regarding the educational opportunities of people with disabilities. Examining how disability is portrayed in society offers a way to understand how the people affecting schools formulate their ideas about individuals with disabilities.

For example, two people, Mary and Bill, are engaged in casual conversation, and the topic turns to autism. Mary says to Bill, "I don't really know a lot about autism. Is it those people with more than one personality?" Bill says, "No, it's like *Rain Man*. You know, the movie with Dustin Hoffman and Tom Cruise. Autism is where they echo things you say, have rigid routines, noise hurts their ears." Mary says, "Oh yeah, I know now, I was just confused. Yes, my neighbor has autism. He's just like *Rain Man*, only he doesn't have any super-duper skills." The conversation goes on about autism and autistic savants. The point here is that two people used a movie to come to common ground about defining a disability and its characteristics. The movie *Rain Man* has left an indelible image on the public regarding the characteristics of autism. Later in the month, Mary was attending a Parent Teacher Student Organization (PTSO) meeting where inclusion was being discussed. Mary argued against inclusion based on her beliefs from viewing the movie *Rain Man* that students with autism are not capable of functioning in the community. She believed, as was shown in the movie, that it was better to keep these students away from too much stimulation. Therefore, she thought that the children with autism at her daughter's school should be isolated from the school community. As we see, Mary voted on what happens to these students based on a movie she saw. This is not uncommon.

Some movies portray individuals with disabilities as being dangerous monsters or disarmingly cute eternal children. This perpetuates segregation and leads to providing different types of educational opportunities for children in schools today. For example, some movies show that people with disabilities need a different type of education, because they are different. Other films portray that "those" kids with disabilities need life skills, not college-prep classes. These media messages influence the hidden curriculum that says "those" kids with disabilities need to be taught different things, in separate settings apart from "the rest of our kids."

SEGREGATION JUSTIFIED

Some exceptional acting performances have been accomplished in depicting cognitively disabled characters, such as Dustin Hoffman in *Rain Man* and Leonardo DiCaprio in *What's Eating Gilbert Grape?* I have intentionally used the term "disabled character" instead of the person-first terminology "character with a disability" to emphasize the point that these characters are not considered to be a person first. In these feature films, they are disabled persons first and foremost. The focus is on how their cognitive disability rules every aspect of their lives. Other facets of their personalities are subordinate to the disability. While there is a parcel of truth in each of the stereotypes presented, these characters are largely one-dimensional; the films do not show a full range of emotions, thoughts, or feelings for the disabled person. The impact of such portrayals is that they reinforce the "us against them" idea so prevalent in society.

My purpose in preparing this analysis is to discuss how these portrayals perpetuate segregation. By focusing on how people with disabilities are different from others, these films can justify differential treatment. Through these images we define ourselves by defining the other. I felt only the following films were appropriate for analysis due to their wide viewing audience and, as a result, potential for influencing public perception. The first name listed for each movie is the actor portraying the disabled character.

- *Of Mice and Men* (1992)—John Malkovich and Gary Sinise (remake of 1939 version with Lon Chaney and Burgess Meredith)
- *To Kill a Mockingbird* (1962)—Robert Duvall and Gregory Peck
- *Tim* (1979)—Mel Gibson and Piper Laurie
- *Dominique and Eugene* (1988)—Tom Hulce, Ray Liotta, and Jamie Lee Curtis
- *Rain Man* (1988)—Dustin Hoffman and Tom Cruise
- *What's Eating Gilbert Grape?* (1993)—Leonardo DiCaprio, Johnny Depp, and Juliette Lewis
- *Forrest Gump* (1994)—Tom Hanks, Robin Wright Penn, Sally Field, and Gary Sinise
- *Sling Blade* (1996)—Billy Bob Thornton, Dwight Yoakam, John Ritter, Lucas Black, and Robert Duvall
- *There's Something about Mary* (1998)—W. Earl Brown, Carmen Diaz, Matt Dillon, Ben Stiller, and Chris Elliott
- *The Other Sister* (1999)—Juliette Lewis, Giovanni Ribisi, Diane Keaton, and Tom Skerritt
- *I Am Sam* (2001)—Sean Penn and Michelle Pfeiffer, plus several characters with developmental disabilities playing Sam's friends
- *Profoundly Normal* (2003, Television)—Kirstie Alley and Delroy Lindo

DANGEROUS MONSTERS

In three films, *To Kill a Mockingbird*, *Of Mice and Men*, and *Sling Blade*, segregation is justified due to the belief that the disabled characters are dangerous monsters. They are not mean-spirited or malicious, but are dangerous because of their cognitive limitations that hamper their understanding of their own strength and potential danger. A major theme of *To Kill a Mockingbird* involves the neighborhood children spying on this anomaly, the dangerous monster, Boo Radley. They watch the house and try to get a peek at the courthouse room where Boo was allegedly chained. The children see him as a dangerous maniac who needs to be locked away in his family home. Even when Boo saves the children's lives and must appear at the police station, he hides in the corner. He blends into the woodwork, hoping to become somewhat invisible. While he craves some kind of contact, as is evidenced by his leaving Jem Finch small trinkets in a knothole, he cannot effectively interact with people. This movie sends a clear message that it is in Boo's best interest to be isolated and alone, without seeing the light of day. Arthur "Boo" Radley is incapable of inclusion in the community.

Lennie, in *Of Mice and Men*, is a kind-hearted man who unquestioningly follows what George tells him to do. He likes to touch soft things, which has resulted in trouble. Near the end of the movie, Lennie touches the hair of the boss's wife, loses himself in the act, and scares her. When she screams, he panics and breaks her neck. He then runs, as the farmhands mount a posse to either shoot him, lynch him, or put him away for good. The message: "better off dead than retarded."

Karl, in *Sling Blade*, is viewed as dangerous because he murders his mother and a neighbor to right wrongs he doesn't fully understand (i.e., he catches his mother having sex with the neighbor). He is freed from the institution after the authorities agree with Karl's perception that, "I reckon I got no reason to kill no one else." Still, he is at a loss in the community, and doesn't fit into society well. He does, however, make friends with a young boy whose mother has an abusive boyfriend. Karl's avenging angel sense of justice returns as he kills again, compelled to right wrongs inflicted on people dear to his heart.

DANGER TO THEMSELVES

In *Rain Man*, Raymond Babbitt gets upset and starts hitting himself when a smoke alarm starts blaring. Before this point, he and his brother, Charlie, have successfully traveled across the United States and even enjoyed several remarkable experiences in Las Vegas, although Charlie is frustrated with Raymond's rigid routines. Still, due to the smoke alarm frightening him and the potential for self-harm, it is decided that for Raymond's own good he should be sent back to the segregated life of the institution rather than living in the community with his brother.

In *What's Eating Gilbert Grape?* Arnie is not allowed to go farther than the front porch of his house unless he is with Gilbert; still, he runs to the town's water tower every chance he gets. He loves climbing the tall ladder; however, he doesn't know how to get down. While his brothers and sisters feel they have to watch him constantly, they continue to accept this incredible burden without question, and feel accompanying guilt each time Arnie runs away (which usually involves the police and rescue personnel). Arnie is eventually taken to jail for climbing the tower. At age 18,

Arnie still does not bathe himself. When Arnie finally says he thinks he can do it, Gilbert sneaks out to see his new girlfriend. When Gilbert returns in the morning, however, Arnie is still in the bathtub, shivering. His mother babies Arnie, and each family member sees him as special and in need of protection that cannot be offered outside of the home.

The common theme among all of these movies is that the characters with cognitive disabilities are portrayed as unable to form "normal" interpersonal relationships and must, therefore, be kept away from society. Community integration is seen as a danger to themselves or others. Therefore, it is most humane to keep them segregated and isolated for the rest of their lives.

CREDULITY AND GULLIBILITY

In *Of Mice and Men*, George tells about how Lennie is always getting into trouble because he's "so damned dumb." He recalls an incident where they got Lennie to jump into the river even though he could not swim. When George saved Lennie from drowning, he was so grateful that he forgot it was George who told him to jump. Lennie looks to George for continual guidance. When he looks at the boss's wife, George reprimands him severely, telling him that a woman like that will only get him into trouble; thus reinforcing the message that Lennie's gullibility is a liability for both of them.

TARGET OF PRACTICAL JOKES

In *There's Something about Mary*, Mary's brother, Warren, is happy only when he is around his family or other individuals with mental retardation. Mary is continually defending Warren against cruel practical jokes inflicted upon him by nondisabled peers. In the opening scene of the movie, Warren is looking for his baseball. Some boys tell him that a girl nearby has his ball, but she calls it a wiener, and he should go ask her for it. This results in Warren being pushed around by the girl's boyfriend.

In *A Simple Plan*, Jacob shares his desire to have a girlfriend and eventually a family. He believes that since they now have money (which they found in a crashed airplane), he might be able to make this wish come true. His brother states that it doesn't take money to have a girlfriend, and reminds Jacob that he had a girlfriend in high school. Jacob then tells how that was all a practical joke. Carrie Richards's friends bet her $100 that she wouldn't go steady with Jacob for a month. He wistfully recalls how she even let him hold her hand until he perspired too much and had to let go. He was grateful to her because she would say "hi" to him once the month was over. He states, "That was cool, she didn't have to do that."

EASY MARK, UNSUSPECTING DUPE

Dominique, "Niki," in *Dominique and Eugene*, makes deliveries for a drug dealer whom he trusts as his friend. His brother, Eugene, finds out and confronts the drug dealer, who asks him if he is a "retard, too." Niki's innocence and helpful nature make him an easy mark for exploitation. Gullibility has been cited as a characteristic of mental retardation. However, gullibility is not the only trait of those with cognitive disabilities; their entire existence does not revolve around being a target.

NO RECIPROCAL PEER RELATIONSHIPS

Two movies in particular, *Rain Man* and *What's Eating Gilbert Grape?* show disabled characters without reciprocal peer relationships. The characters have no interactions with peers, with or without disabilities. Their only social encounters are with family members (or in the case of *Rain Man*, his paid care providers). One scene in *What's Eating Gilbert Grape?* shows Arnie at the opening of a fast food restaurant—a big event in town. He asks several young people there to attend his birthday party, although he's never met them. Gilbert notices that Arnie is talking to others and quickly rescues him. There is no mention of Arnie going to school or even leaving the house, except for when he runs away or goes to work with Gilbert at the local store.

These characters are completely isolated from the community and other people. Family members in these films accept these conditions without challenge. It is understood that the disabled character does not want or need human contact outside of the family. Assuming that individuals with cognitive disabilities are conspicuously different from the rest of us who are social beings is dangerous and perpetuates segregation and isolation.

BEST FRIENDS ARE CHILDREN

In both *Sling Blade* and *Dominique and Eugene*, the disabled characters develop friendships with young boys. In *Sling Blade*, Karl makes friends with young Frank. When Karl goes to Frank's house for the first time, he waits outside for two hours until someone comes to the door. He did not know, or was afraid, to knock. Karl and Frank look after each other. Frank provides Karl with access to the community, and Karl protects Frank from his mother's abusive boyfriend. In *Dominique and Eugene*, Niki's garbage truck coworker teases him about his friendship with young Mikee, stating, "You finally found someone with the same IQ to be friends with." Mikee had an abusive father who ends up killing him by pushing him down the stairs. Niki witnesses the event and brings the father to justice through the help of his brother, Eugene. In both movies, the disabled character feels more comfortable with a young, vulnerable, and abused child than with his same-age peers. However, given his adult status, the disabled character feels a sense of duty to protect his best friend.

BENEFACTOR RELATIONSHIPS

In *Tim*, the main character is infantilized, as the audience views the development of his interpersonal relationship with an older woman, Mary, who serves as his benefactor. He has no friends in the community, only caretakers. Tim works on a yard crew with several young men who always leave him to do the clean up. They definitely do not see him as a peer, but rather as someone to do the dirty work for them. Mary marries him after his mother dies and his father becomes despondent. However, this relationship is more reflective of a parent–child relationship than an equal partnership. In *Forrest Gump*, while Forrest is eternally in love with Jenny, his childhood friend, her love for him is paternalistic. She sees him as the safe eternal child who will not hurt her like the adult men in her life. And finally, in *Of Mice and Men*, George has cared for Lennie since the death of his aunt Clara. They talk about being each other's only family members. George protects Lennie, and Lennie obediently follows his lead. These films distinctly show dependent relationships without the reciprocal interpersonal exchanges that are valued in most people's lives.

HINDERS FAMILY MEMBERS FROM HAVING INTIMATE RELATIONSHIPS

Two films, *What's Eating Gilbert Grape?* and *Dominique and Eugene*, depict the limitations placed on family members due to caring for the disabled sibling. *What's Eating Gilbert Grape?* focuses on the burden three young people bear due to a brother with mental retardation and a mother who weighs 500 pounds and hasn't left the house in more than seven years. Early in the movie, Gilbert states, "Some days I want him to live, some days I don't." This burden on Gilbert negatively affects his ability to develop a relationship with a young girl he meets. In *Dominique and Eugene*, Eugene is accepted into Stanford for a medical internship, but wonders if he can accept it because he cannot leave his brother. He also develops an interest in a young woman, but the relationship is impeded by his need to constantly care for his brother. In both of these movies, the brothers of the disabled characters frequently refer to them as "good boy." The siblings also mention repeatedly, "I can't take care of you every minute." This characterization of dependency evokes pity for the sibling, but serves to reinforce stereotypes that erect barriers to community integration and independent living.

DISARMINGLY CUTE ETERNAL CHILDREN

Films that have been described as creating more positive portrayals, such as *Forrest Gump* and *The Other Sister*, depict characters who lead storybook lives with incredible luck (rather than skills of their own) interceding to allow integration into the community. This reinforces the notion of a child trapped in an adult body. Three films in particular—*The Other Sister, Rain Man,* and *Tim*—portray the disabled character as a sweet, innocent, cute eternal child. In *The Other Sister*, Carla and Daniel (her boyfriend with mental retardation) are inexperienced in typical behaviors for their age, such as dating. They are attending college, but giggle when they see people their own age drinking and kissing. They are cute, naive, and silly. In *Rain Man*, Raymond's endearing qualities are evidenced nearly 15 years after the film's debut, when someone affectionately repeats one of his lines from the movie, such as "I'm an excellent driver." The innocent, fragile, Raymond Babbitt has become one of "America's Sweethearts." However, there is little dialogue regarding how Raymond could fit into the community. Discussion focuses more on joking about his savant tendencies and inability to break out of routines. Finally, we find Tim cute and lovable as he asks Mary, "What is dying?" and tells her how he loves her "as much as his mum and dad," but more than his sister. His childlike innocence is highlighted again and again as he tries to express emotions. The audience truly sees Tim as someone to be taken in, nurtured, and protected.

NO NONDISABLED FRIENDS

In *I Am Sam*, the main character has several friends from a work program for people with mental retardation. Nevertheless, Sam is seen by the community as unable to care for a seven-year-old daughter, even with the help of social service agencies. He has not made friends with nondisabled coworkers at Starbucks. He has not made friends in his neighborhood or with parents of his daughter's schoolmates. However, one especially positive feature of this film is the use of actors with cognitive disabilities to fill the roles of Sam's friends. I hope this trend will continue. It greatly added to the movie to show the loyalty and strength of the bonds that had formed between five young men with mental retardation who kept in regular contact after being placed in community employment.

In *The Other Sister*, Carla Tate does develop one meaningful relationship with a boy who also has mental retardation. While it is commendable that the story shows two people with mental retardation attending community college, it shows them as being very different from their peers. Without each other, they would have no same-age friends. The relationships that Carla has with her family and Daniel has with a neighbor who watches after him form the entirety of their social networks.

SUMMARY

Although the media have made huge advances in portrayals of persons with disabilities in such films as *Notting Hill*, television shows including *Joan of Arcadia* and *West Wing*, and even commercials, current portrayals in popular media do not strive to enhance opportunities for community integration and the development of interpersonal relationships for those with cognitive disabilities. These images often reinforce stereotypes in our culture that individuals with cognitive disabilities need to be "protected from" same-age peers because they are either dangerous or cognitively unable to handle interpersonal relationships without more capable benefactors moderating and intervening on their behalf. These messages influence school policies, curricula, and more importantly, expectations of educators. It is important, then, that these subtle messages are brought to light so that more equitable opportunities exist for all students. Nondisabled students need to learn that individuals with cognitive disabilities are capable of much more than previously thought possible. And students with cognitive disabilities need to have social and educational opportunities that are integrated and equitable. Together, we must change public perception before we can end the isolation.

Images of Disability in Literature

Cynthia Ann Bowman and Paul T. Jaeger

INTRODUCTION

Disability has been represented in art for thousands of years. Many types of media include images of disability, such as painting, sculpture, television, print advertising, and innumerable other forms of expression. This chapter, however, focuses on how disability is depicted in literature, which allows us to gain insight into the perceptions and attitudes of society in ways otherwise restricted or impossible.

DISABILITY AND LITERATURE

Tiny Tim, Helen Keller, and Captain Hook, three seemingly unrelated characters of popular literature, have a prominent common characteristic: a disability. Tiny Tim has brought tears to the eyes of young and old as he faced the adversity of hobbling around on crutches at such a tender age while enthusiastically exclaiming, "God bless us every one!" The true and oft-retold story of Helen Keller has inspired many people who watched her face deafness, blindness, and underestimation on her way to brilliance. We have scorned that bitter, scheming captain with a hook for a hand as he attempted to bring demise to the ever-magical boy in green tights. If you let these three legendary characters swirl in your brain for a minute, you just might be able to relive the heartbreaking innocence and irony of Tiny Tim's blessing, the feeling of general good as Helen Keller finally achieved the fame she so richly deserved, and the deep hatred for the despicable, evil Captain Hook. What you likely won't realize is the typical stereotypes that these characters have been fulfilling in the media for decades on end—disabled innocence (Tiny Tim), disabled inspiration (Helen Keller), and disabled evil (Captain Hook).

The portrayal of persons with disabilities in literature and mass media has been varied, though often negative. Inappropriate information has engendered attitudes ranging from feelings of pity or revulsion to expectations of superhuman powers of intellect or insight. "Disability is a significant means of social differentiation in modern societies" (Barton, 1996, p. 13). When disability is represented artistically, it can be based on imagination, stereotypes, personal experience as a person with a disability, or the experiences of friends, family members, or caregivers with disabilities. Sometimes a certain aspect of living with a disability is the subject of the literature. The work of art may focus on acquiring a changed identity or moving with this identity into a new life experience.

In literature, disability may be incorporated as part of the life experiences that are either central or peripheral for the character in the work. Often, the disability marks the character as a foil or as a representative of weakness and evil or unearthly purity, pathos, spirituality, and self-abnegation. The dominant social attitude views "disability in medical and psychological terms" (Barton, 1996, p. 6). Medical and psychological values and interpretations, given a great deal of social import, have emphasized the impairment over the identity of the individual (Rieser & Mason, 1990), which is often reflected in portrayals of disability. There is literature about disability in every cultural medium, genre, and subgenre, and the subject been treated from every possible perspective—as stigma, divine challenge, divine punishment, defeat, part of everyday life, and opportunity or challenge.

In representing those with disabilities, writers often veer between competing impulses toward idealization and stigmatization. Through history, individuals with disabilities have been locked away against their will in prisons, asylums, and monasteries; they have been considered witches; and they have been thought to suffer from demonic possession (Bragg, 1997). That attitude has resulted in individuals with disabilities being killed, exiled, neglected, shunned, used for entertainment, or even treated as spiritual manifestations, both good and evil (Hewett, 1974).

Varying cultural meanings of disability have reflected the historical/social contexts. For example, in much "postapocalyptic" science fiction, those who are disabled or born mutated because of radiation exposure are most often represented as the enemies, the "others," the source of conflict or danger to be overcome by the survivors. They are the "bad guys," like the crippled king in Shakespeare's *Richard III*. By examining how individuals with disabilities are portrayed in artistic representations, such as literature, we will be able to gain a greater appreciation of the historical evolution of social perceptions of disability. This allows for a better understanding of how to bring disability into the social mainstream, so that it is seen as an aspect of diversity rather than as a stigmatizing impairment. Scholars who study disability issues have created a number of perspectives for examining the subject.

LITERARY REPRESENTATIONS OF DISABILITY THROUGH HISTORY

Examined below are works of literature through history that prominently represent disability. This is by no means a comprehensive cataloguing of literary depictions of disability. Instead, it is an examination of certain, particularly revealing historical works that are often taught in high school English or Language Arts classes, and discussed in terms of social perceptions, as well as legal, medical, and educational contexts from the time they were originally written.

Oedipus Rex (Sophocles, first performed in 430 BCE)

Laius, ruler of Thebes, is told by an oracle that his son will kill him. With the agreement of his wife, Jocasta, the baby's feet are pinioned and the baby is given to a slave to be "exposed" on nearby Mount Cithaeron (haunt of wolves and other wild beasts). The slave, a shepherd of Laius's flocks, takes pity on the baby, and instead of leaving him to die, gives the boy to a fellow shepherd from Corinth, the other side of the mountain. The Corinthian shepherd presents the baby to the childless king of Corinth, Polybus, who brings him up as his own, presumably giving him the name "Oedipus" (Swollen Foot) because of his deformity.

At the height of civilization in ancient Greece and Rome, it was socially acceptable to abandon babies born with disabilities, tied or staked down on sunny hillsides, so as to perish in the sun (Garland, 1995). In Rome, children with visual impairments were often trained as beggars, and the girls were frequently sold into prostitution (French, 1932). Wealthy Roman households sometimes purchased individuals with mental impairments to serve as amusement (Kanner, 1964).

Of a Monstrous Child (Montaigne, first published in approximately 1580)

In this essay, Montaigne describes two children joined together at birth in a heartbreakingly graphic manner and the family who planned to capitalize on this "strangeness" for financial gain. "Under his paps he was fastned and joyned to another childe, but had no head, and who had the conduite of his backe stopped; the rest whole. One of his armes was shorter than the other, and was by accident broken at their birth. They were joyned face to face, and as if a little child would embrace another somewhat bigger [spelling in original]."

Prior to the eighteenth century, individuals with disabilities were usually allowed into society only if "under supervision" (Stiker, 1999, p. 69). If not supported by their family, often they were forced to beg to survive because they were not allowed or given the chance to have jobs. Begging became so important to people with disabilities in the Middle Ages that guilds and brotherhoods of beggars with disabilities were created (Covey, 1998).

Richard III (Shakespeare, first performed in 1597)

Shakespeare based his portrait of Richard on information found in histories written by Edward Hall, Raphael Holinshed, and Sir Thomas More. Drawing on this historical data, he created a dramatic character from one of the most unusual figures in the fifteenth-century Wars of the Roses. Richard III was England's last king to die in battle. Holinshed's histories gave a biased description of Richard, stressing his supposed physical deformity and depicting him as arrogant, hypocritical, cruel, and ambitious. To serve his own dramatic needs, Shakespeare refined and embellished the available historical material. His Richard becomes a fully developed character, who is both the victim of circumstances and the commander of his own destiny. This conflict is the force that most critics feel gives the play its special energy and fascination. Shakespeare exposes Richard's wit, his psychological understanding of others, and the evil record of his victims, inviting the reader to consider how much Richard himself may be a victim—of his nature, his circumstances, his deformed body, and the past in general. Shakespeare's greatest challenge was to inspire a response to the notorious Richard—his wicked deeds, his charisma, and such names as "Foul Devil," "Lump of foul deformity," "Bottled spider," "Cacodemon," and "Poisonous hunch-backed toad."

Around the time that Shakespeare was writing, the belief that a disability was unquestionably a manifestation of divine punishment was becoming popular in England and its colonies (Covey, 1998). In fact, individuals with disabilities in colonial America were often forced out of towns and even sometimes sent back to Europe (Shapiro, 1993). The perception of disability as heavenly wrath was popularized by many of the same people who also advocated the burning of people who were accused of witchcraft (Covey, 1998; Winship, 1994).

Of Deformity (Bacon, first published in 1625)

Like many writers throughout history, Bacon struggled with the causes/ effects of disability: "Deformed persons are commonly even with nature;

for as nature hath done ill by them, so do they by nature; being for the most part (as the Scripture saith) void of natural affection; and so they have their revenge of nature . . . Therefore it is good to consider deformity, not as a sign, which is more deceivable; but as a cause, which seldom faileth of the effect. Whosoever hath anything fixed in his person, that doth induce contempt, hath also a perpetual spur in himself, to rescue and deliver himself from scorn. Therefore all deformed persons, are extreme bold . . . So that upon the matter, in a great wit, deformity is an advantage to rising . . . Still the ground is, they will, if they be of spirit, seek to free themselves from scorn; which must be either by virtue or malice; and therefore let it not be marvelled, if sometimes they prove excellent persons."

Many efforts were made to make people with disabilities invisible to society at large. Individuals with certain impairments, such as mental disorders and epilepsy, were often locked away in asylums, madhouses, and prisons, while those with Hansen's disease (leprosy) were forced to live in isolated camps, with Europe having as many as 19,000 leprosy villages at one time (Foucault, 1965; Braddock & Parish, 2001). People with disabilities were also commonly sent to sea where they would be away from the community or could be dropped off in some other population where the ship landed (Foucault, 1965). Both John Calvin and Martin Luther advocated the belief that individuals with mental disabilities were created by Satan (Braddock & Parish, 2001). In Renaissance times (1300–1500), it was common to beat individuals with mental or cognitive disabilities on the head as a way to treat their affliction (Braddock & Parish, 2001).

On His Blindness (Milton, first published in approximately 1660)

> When I consider how my light is spent
> Ere half my days in this dark world and wide,
> And that one Talent which is death to hide
> Lodged with me useless . . .

Milton struggled with the onset of blindness, questioning his self-worth as he lost his ability to see his words on paper, and seeking the patience to endure. The Code of Justinian, compiled beginning in 533 CE under orders of Roman emperor Justinian, created a unified code of civil law for the empire that had a tremendous impact on laws of most of Europe until well into the eighteenth century. These laws, and the views they engendered, remained highly influential in Europe well into the later half of the second millennium of the Common Era. Jurists interpreting Roman law were primarily concerned with disability as a cause of actions in legal cases; for example, Roman law allowed the appointment of guardians for individuals with mental illnesses (Gaw, 1906; Gaw, 1907). One curious feature of Roman law was that people with hearing impairments had the right to be citizens only if they could communicate verbally (Gaw, 1906).

The Yellow Wallpaper (Gilman, first published in 1892)

In this classic late nineteenth-century story by Charlotte Perkins Gilman, a new mother suffering from what today we might call postpartum depression is diagnosed with a nervous disorder. Instructed to abandon her intellectual life and avoid stimulating company, she sinks into a still-deeper depression that is invisible to her husband, who believes he knows what is best for her. Alone in the yellow-wallpapered nursery of a rented house, she descends into madness.

The isolation of people with mental disorders has been a common thread throughout history. When The Yellow Wallpaper was written, most states had laws mandating the institutionalization of individuals with various mental disabilities. Students with even mild mental impairments were predominantly denied an education at the time, a situation that persisted for nearly another century. By 1962, only 16 states educated children with mild mental impairments; in the mid-1970s, some states simply did not allow children with cognitive disabilities to attend public schools (Smith, 2001). Those few who did receive an education were primarily in separate residential institutions that were nothing like the schools other students attended (Winzer, 1993). These institutions were "warehouses where people were isolated from society . . . Children with disabilities apparently were not worthy of investment" (Smith, 2001, p. 15). The individuals housed in these residential schools were "confined and isolated rather than aided toward independence" and sheltered from the world they were believed unable to survive (Bryan, 1996, p. 4). Further, "[t]his socially sanctioned segregation reinforced negative societal attitudes toward human difference" (Braddock & Parish, 2001, p. 52).

The Monster (Crane, first published in 1899)

A black man saves a small-town doctor's son from a burning house. In gratitude, the doctor takes it upon himself to salvage the life of the badly burned and disfigured hero. Others warn him that he is doing no service to the patient, but the physician cannot let go of one to whom he owes such a profound debt. The town begins to fear the newly created "monster." The burned man's life becomes a nightmare of rejection, while the community progressively spurns the physician and his family.

Most attempts by parents to gain the right of education for their children with disabilities were soundly and callously rejected by the courts, often for reasons that involved the perceptions and appearances of these children rather than their ability to learn or interact with others. In 1893, the Supreme Judicial Court of Massachusetts permitted the state to expel a student who seemed "weak in mind" (*Watson v. City of Cambridge*, 1893). In 1919, the Wisconsin Supreme Court held that a child who drooled, had a speech impediment, and suffered facial contortions should not be allowed into public schools, in spite of the fact that the student had demonstrated the ability to academically and physically benefit from an education (*Beattie v. Board of Education of City of Antigo*, 1919). In both of these cases, appearances played a significant part in the decision to prevent the child from attending school.

The Sound and the Fury (Faulkner, first published in 1929)

The subject of *The Sound and the Fury* is the dissolution of the Compsons, an old Mississippi family that fell on hard times after the Civil War. This dark, scandal-ridden story of squandered fortune, madness, congenital brain damage, theft, illegitimacy, and stoic endurance is told in the interior voices of three Compson brothers: Benjy, the "idiot" man-child who blurs together three decades of inchoate sensations as he stalks the fringes of the family's former pasture; Quentin, torturing himself obsessively over his sister and his own failure to recover the family's honor as he wanders around the seedy fringes of Boston; and Jason, heartless, shrewd, sneaking, and nursing a perpetual sense of injury and outrage against his family.

In the novel, Benjy is castrated due to his mental illness, which was an outgrowth of the eugenics movement. Sir Francis Galton founded a movement known as eugenics, which was based on the principle that only certain people had the right to have children. In 1914, 38 of the 49 states, territories, and the District of Columbia had laws prohibiting marriage for individuals with disabilities, either completely or until the woman was past childbearing age (Smith, Wilkinson & Wagoner, 1914). The U.S. Supreme Court upheld the validity of these laws (*Buck v. Bell*, 1927).

Children of a Lesser God (Medoff, first published in 1980)

This play depicts the struggle of a woman with a hearing impairment for acceptance in a hearing world. "It is a silence full of sound." This story evidences a great deal about the various issues related to sign language, in which the two main characters argue over lip-reading as opposed to signing. This debate gains significantly from an understanding of the origins of attempts to create ways for people with hearing impairments to communicate.

The earliest known form of sign language was created around 1510, and these early methods of teaching inspired the creation of residential schools for people with hearing and, later, visual impairments, offering the first formal education for individuals with disabilities (Daniels, 1997; Winzer, 1997). By the early 1800s, many European nations were offering private, and sometimes even public, education to children with a wide range of disabilities (Winzer, 1993). In France, students with hearing impairments were first schooled in 1748 (Winzer, 1993). In the United States, President Lincoln signed into law the bill creating Gallaudet College, for individuals with hearing disabilities, in 1864. However, children with hearing impairments who were receiving an education still faced tremendous discrimination within their own schools. "Teachers at the end of the century spoke of making deaf children more like 'normal' people and less like savages by forbidding them the use of sign language, and they opposed deaf marriages with a rhetoric of evolutionary progress and decline" (Baynton, 2001, p. 36).

Freak the Mighty (Philbrick, first published in 1993)

This is the story of an extraordinary friendship between Kevin ("Freak"), a brilliant 12-year-old whose birth defect prevents growth, and gigantic Max, who can barely read, making school an ordeal. Since his dad's in jail for killing his mother, Max lives with gentle Gram and the aptly named Grim in a fairly rough neighborhood. When Kevin perches on Max's shoulders, they call themselves "Freak the Mighty." The two have much to give each other—with Freak's quick wit and Max's long legs, they explore the neighborhood and beat a gang of bullies. Freak, with his vast vocabulary and imagination to match, gets Max involved in his elaborate fantasy games and lures him into reading. When school starts, Max is placed in the gifted class to help his friend. Max's description of their friendship—written after Freak's death, in the blank book that Freak had given him—is gritty, unsentimental, and poignant.

This story embodies the educational progress made in society for students with disabilities following the passage of disability rights laws. The Individuals with Disabilities Education Act mandates the public education of all school-age individuals with disabilities (20 U.S.C.A. § 1400 et seq.), guaranteeing a free appropriate public education to these students through their high school graduation. Part of this set of protections is equal access to the benefits of public schooling. Students with disabilities have the right to be educated in an integrated setting to the maximum extent feasible and to have a program of learning designed to fit their individual needs and capabilities. In this story, Max and Freak benefit not only from each other's friendship, but also from the right to be educated in an inclusive setting. Had this story occurred merely a couple of decades earlier, it is entirely possible that neither of the main characters would even have been allowed to attend school.

The Autobiography of a Face (Grealy, first published in 1994)

Poet Lucy Grealy tells the story of her childhood and young adulthood, a 20-year period of overwhelming physical and mental suffering. At age nine, first misdiagnosed and finally identified as having facial bone cancer (Ewing's sarcoma), Lucy underwent several surgeries and more than two years of intensive chemotherapy and radiation treatments. Pain and nausea, and the anxiety and fear of having more pain and nausea were only part of the ordeal. Lucy became aware of what it is to be severely, chronically ill. Her sisters behaved differently toward her. "Suddenly I understood the term visiting. I was in one place, they were in another, and they were only pausing." Being at home was worse than being in the hospital. In the hospital, she felt no guilt or shame; however, amidst her family, she blamed herself for the tension, arguments over money, and her mother's depression. Her hair fell out, and she became aware that people were staring at her face. Nevertheless, she felt "naturally adept at protecting myself from the hurt of their insults and felt a vague superiority."

At school, Lucy's disfigured face drew taunts from classmates; she understood that she was perceived as ugly. Her moods alternated between despair, determination, and escapism. She became convinced that only facial reconstruction and a restored appearance would make life bearable. During years of reconstructive surgery, Lucy evolved complex rationalizations to give meaning to her suffering. Two anchors had stabilized her existence throughout the misery: a passionate adolescent love of horses and an adult love of poetry. Eventually, outward appearance and inner life became harmonious. "The journey back to my face was a long one."

This story reveals much about the inner struggles of and external challenges for children with disabilities. Grealy addresses many of the topics touched upon by other pieces of literature that we have already discussed: exclusion, shunning as a result of appearance, placement in facilities away from others, alienation in education, and the stress of disability on the family. This story is imminently teachable for representations of disability, however, because all of these issues are seamlessly incorporated into a discussion of her life. As it is autobiographical, Grealy recounts her problems in society, medicine, and education, as well as her own self-doubts, in terms of herself as a complete person. Ultimately, in her own life, she overcomes the difficulties that have historically plagued individuals with disabilities.

CONCLUSION

This chapter presents a range of the ways in which disability has been depicted in literature throughout history (for further suggested fictional works related to disabilities, please see Appendix I). It is very important to understand these varying representations because they provide insight into how disability has been perceived through the years and reveal changes in social attitudes toward individuals with disabilities.

These texts also disclose the types of representations of disability that may be encountered in material assigned in high school courses. How disability is conveyed in literature can have an effect on readers, potentially shaping how they view people with disabilities. It is important to keep in mind when reading literature that outdated, unfair, or simply biased portrayals of individuals with disabilities may be encountered. Being aware of this possibility means that such portrayals, and any misconceptions that they engender in others, will not come as a complete surprise. Such situations can be viewed as an opportunity to educate other students, and possibly even teachers, regarding what an actual person with a disability feels about outdated or unfair representations in literature. It is an important challenge!

REFERENCES

Abberly, P. (1987). The concept of oppression and the development of a social theory of disability. *Disability, Handicap and Society, 2*, 5–20.

Albrecht, G.L. (1992). *The disability business: Rehabilitation in America*. Newbury Park, CA: Sage Publications.

Bacon, F. (1985). *The essays*. New York: Penguin Books.

Barnes, C. (1990). *Cabbage syndrome: The social construction of dependence*. Lewes, UK: Falmer.

Barton, L. (1996). Sociology and disability: Some emerging issues. In L. Barton (Ed.), *Disability and society: Emerging issues and insights* (pp. 3–17). London: Addison Wesley Longman Ltd.

Baynton, D.C. (2001). Disability and the justification of inequality in American history. In P.K. Longmore & L. Umansky (Eds.), *The new disability history: American perspectives* (pp. 33–57). New York: New York University Press.

Beattie v. Board of Education of City of Antigo, 172 N.W. 153 (Wis. 1919).

Braddock, D.L. & Parish, S.L. (2001). An institutional history of disability. In G.L. Albrecht, K.D. Seelman & M. Bury (Eds.), *Handbook of disability studies* (pp. 351–372). Thousand Oaks, CA: Sage Publications.

Bragg, L. (1997). From the mute god to the lesser god: Disability in medieval Celtic and Old Norse literature. *Disability & Society, 12*, 165–177.

Bryan, W.V. (1996). *In search of freedom: How persons with disabilities have been disenfranchised from the mainstream of American society*. Springfield, IL: Charles C. Thomas Publisher.

Buck v. Bell, 274 U.S. 200 (1927).

Christensen, C. (1996). Disabled, handicapped or disordered: "What's in a name?" In C. Christensen & F. Rizvi (Eds.), *Disability and the dilemmas of education and justice* (pp. 63–78). Buckingham: Open University Press.

Corker, M. & French, S. (Eds.). (1999). *Disability discourse*. Buckingham: Open University Press.

Covey, H.C. (1998). *Social perceptions of people with disabilities in history*. Springfield, IL: Charles C. Thomas.

Crane, S. (1987). *Great short works of Stephen Crane:* Red badge of courage, Monster, Maggie, Open boat, Blue hotel, Bride comes to Yellow Sky *and other works*. New York: HarperCollins.

Daniels, M. (1997). *Benedictine roots in the development of deaf education: Listening with the heart*. Westport, CT: Bergin & Garvey.

Edwards, M.L. (1997). Deaf and dumb in ancient Greece. In L. Davis (Ed.), *The disability studies reader* (pp. 29–51). New York: Routledge.

Faulkner, W. (1967). *The sound and the fury*. New York: McGraw-Hill.

Foucault, M. (1965). *Madness and civilization: A history of insanity in the age of reason* (R. Howard, trans.). New York: Vintage Books.

French, R.S. (1932). *From Homer to Helen Keller: A social and educational study of the blind*. New York: American Foundation for the Blind.

Garland, R. (1995). *The eye of the beholder: Deformity and disability in the Graeco-Roman world*. Ithaca, NY: Cornell University Press.

Gaw, A. (1906). The development of the legal status of the deaf. *American Annals of the Deaf, 51,* 269–275, 401–423.

———. (1907). The development of the legal status of the deaf. *American Annals of the Deaf, 52,* 1–12, 167–183, 229–245.

Gilman, C.P. (1997). *The yellow wallpaper*. New York: Dover.

Grealy, L. (2003). *Autobiography of a face*. New York: HarperCollins.

Hewett, F. (1974). *Education of exceptional learners*. Boston: Allyn and Bacon.

Individuals with Disabilities Education Act (IDEA), 20 U.S.C.A § 1400 et seq.

Kanner, L. (1964). *A history of the care and study of the mentally retarded*. Springfield, IL: Charles C. Thomas Publisher.

Kitchen, R. (2000). The researched opinions on research: Disabled people and disability research. *Disability & Society, 15,* 25–47.

Marks, D. (1999). *Disability: Controversial debates and psychological perspectives*. New York: Routledge.

Medoff, M. (1998). *Children of a lesser god*. New York: Dramatist's Play Service.

Milton, J. (1961). *Poems: Selections*. Englewood Cliffs, NJ: Prentice-Hall.

Montaigne, M. (1998). *The complete essays*. New York: Penguin.

Oliver, M. (1990). *The politics of disablement*. London: Macmillan.

Philbrick, R. (2001). *Freak the mighty*. New York: Scholastic.

Riddell, S. (1996). Theorising special education needs in a changing political climate. In L. Barton (Ed.), *Disability and society: Emerging issues and insights* (pp. 83–106). London: Addison Wesley Longman Ltd.

Rieser, R. & Mason, M. (1990). *Disability, equality in the classroom: A human rights issue*. London: ILEA.

Rioux, M. (1994). Towards a concept of equality of well-being: Overcoming the social and legal construction of inequality. In M.H. Rioux & M. Bach (Eds.), *Disability is not measles* (pp. 67–108). North York, Ontario: Roeher Institute.

Rosen, G. (1968). *Madness in society: Chapters in the historical sociology of mental illness*. Chicago: University of Chicago Press.

Shakespeare, T.S. (1994). Cultural representations of disabled people: Dustbins for disavowal. *Disability & Society, 9*(3), 283–301.

Shakespeare, W. (1954). *Richard III*. Cambridge: Cambridge University Press.

Shapiro, J.P. (1993). *No pity: People with disabilities forging a new civil rights movement*. New York: Times Books.

Smith, D.D. (2001). *Special education: Teaching in an age of opportunity*. Boston: Allyn & Bacon.

Smith, S., Wilkinson, M.W. & Wagoner, L.C. (1914). *A summary of the laws of the several states governing marriage and divorce of the feebleminded, epileptic and the insane; asexualization; and institutional commitment and discharge of the feebleminded and the epileptic*. Seattle: University of Washington.

Sophocles, E. (1993). *Oedipus Rex*. London: Dover Publications.

Stiker, H. (1999). *A history of disability* (W. Sayers, Trans.). Ann Arbor, MI: University of Michigan Press.

Stone, D.A. (1984). *The disabled state*. London: Macmillan.

Stone, E. & Priestly, M. (1996). Parasites, prawns and partners: Disability research and the role of non-disabled researchers. *British Journal of Sociology, 47*, 699–716.

Thomas, C. (1999). *Female forms: Experiencing and understanding disability*. Buckingham: Open University Press.

Ward, M. (2002). *Voices from the margins: An annotated bibliography of fiction on disabilities and differences for young people*. Westport, CT: Greenwood Press.

Warkany, J. (1959). Congenital malformations in the past. *Journal of Chronic Disabilities, 10*, 84–96.

Watson v. City of Cambridge, 32 N.E. 864 (Mass. 1893).

Watson, A. (Ed.). (1998). *The digest of Justinian*. 2 vols. Philadelphia: University of Pennsylvania Press.

Winship, M.P. (1994). Prodigies, Puritanism, and the perils of natural philosophy: The example of Cotton Mather. *The William & Mary Quarterly, 51*, 92–105.

Winzer, M.A. (1993). *The history of special education: From isolation to integration*. Washington, DC: Gallaudet University Press.

———. (1997). Disability and society: Before the eighteenth century. In L.J. Davis (Ed.), *The disability studies reader* (pp. 75–109). New York: Routledge.

SECTION III

Interactions and Relationships

INTRODUCTION

The chapters in this section discuss the wide variety of social interactions that occur during the course of a normal day in high school from the perspective of students with disabilities. From getting to classes to finding people to sit with at lunch, these students face unique situations when it comes to the social experiences of high school. This section examines and offers guidance about their unique experiences as they build friendships, work with teachers, attend social events, and go on dates. Information is also offered relating to the special circumstances of students with disabilities who are in gifted programs or doing other kinds of advanced course work. The chapter on extracurricular activities details how having a disability may affect participation in activities, such as school plays and organizations and clubs. Just like all other high school students, individuals with disabilities wish to participate in extracurricular activities.

This section will help high school students with disabilities understand that they are not alone or unusual, be aware of many of the interpersonal issues that they will face, have a strong sense of confidence, knowledge, and empowerment in facing those issues, and be advocates for their own rights. The chapters in this section will help each student with a disability understand that he or she is not alone or unusual. All high school students with disabilities encounter many similar issues, and these chapters will help provide the knowledge and empowerment to deal with the interpersonal issues.

Sight and Insight: My Life in Public School

David W. Hartman

After being sighted for eight years of my childhood, I lost my sight completely. My family, being very naive as to what a visually impaired child might require, enrolled me in Overbrook School for the Blind in Philadelphia. I attended this specialized school for the following five years, where I learned to read Braille, to be mobile in a sightless world, and to socialize with other disabled students. Knowing that I would eventually have to live in a sighted world, when I was in the eighth grade, my parents and I decided that I should enroll in the local public school.

This transition from a school for the blind to a regular public school was made somewhat easier because I spent the summer taking a math course that was taught in the same building where I would be taking classes in the fall. That summer I was able to learn my way around the large middle school campus without having to deal with the usual crowded environment. I was also able to begin the adjustment of dealing with a classroom in which I was the only blind student; for example, I had to get someone to read textbooks to me, and I had to figure out how to hand in my homework to the math teacher in a form he could understand. I discovered early on that I must communicate with my teacher and educate him to my special needs. Together we learned that typing up my math problems was too time consuming and unproductive. Doing the work in Braille proved to be more efficient because I could read my Braille material to the teacher after class.

LIFE INSIDE THE CLASSROOM

When the school year started in the fall, I felt more confident about the process of adapting to a sighted school. Books were obtained through a national organization called Recordings for the Blind, now called Recordings for the Blind and Dyslexic. I would provide this nonprofit organization with two copies of the textbooks I needed, and they would arrange for volunteer readers to record the books onto a reel-to-reel recorder. Today the process is similar, but the material is recorded onto a CD, which allows the student to search the material quickly on a computer or on other specialized equipment. Unfortunately, obtaining the right text to be recorded was never easy; sometimes the teacher made last-minute changes or depended more heavily on handouts, which were provided each week in class. I coped with these last-minute changes by having my mother or other students read for me. Today, computers enable blind students to scan printed material and respond quickly to unexpected changes.

As I progressed through high school, I often depended on my mom to help me with the reading. She spent many hours either reading directly to me or tape-recording the reading material. One time when I was listening to one of her recordings, I realized that she had actually fallen asleep while reading. Somehow, she was able to continue. I have since learned about automatic behavior, which can occur when people fall asleep. Mom was such a great reader that she could continue to read even when in a drowsy state.

Teachers who used the blackboard often complicated my life in the public school classroom. Generally, when they wrote extensive notes on the board, they would not verbalize what they were writing. I felt embarrassed to ask teachers to read aloud what they were writing. However, on one occasion, other students pleaded with me to ask our teacher to read what she was writing on the blackboard. When I asked them what the problem was, they told me that the teacher's handwriting was awful, but they were uncomfortable complaining about it. They thought I could help solve the problem if I would raise the issue.

As a result of this episode, I discovered that asking teachers to be aware of my blindness when they were teaching the class also benefited other students. Later, when I was in medical school, a professor developed a model to illustrate a concept for me. To his surprise and mine, the model helped sighted students understand the material much better. In some cases, my classmates would explain visual material to me; we discovered that students who were willing to take time to help me actually learned the content more fully themselves. In several cases, students who assisted me got better grades as a result of their efforts.

LIFE OUTSIDE THE CLASSROOM

Over time, the process of adapting to the sighted classroom and managing the mechanics of making the written word accessible to me was working. However, integrating into the students' social gatherings was quite a different story. Often I would arrive in class on a Monday morning and overhear students discussing the weekend parties to which I was never invited. Classmates were glad to help me get from class to class and to socialize with me during the school day, but they were reluctant to invite me to their weekend get-togethers or to have fun with me outside the school environment. Though I was able to achieve good grades, I felt that I was failing in my social life.

In order to feel more included in the student body, and in the hopes that I would be viewed in a more normal light, I went out for the wrestling team. Having been on a wrestling team at Overbrook, I had an advantage because I had been wrestling for four or five years; most of my teammates in the public school, in contrast, were just starting their experience in the sport. I was able to make the team, and while I did not win all my matches, I excelled and handled myself well as a wrestler. In this way, I was able to erase my once pathetic image of myself as a blind student and to give others a better idea of who I really was.

My emotional life had many ups and downs as a teenager. I remember once when a girl came up to me and said that a cheerleader wanted to meet me. I thought I had died and gone to heaven. I met the cheerleader and subsequently asked her out. She told me that she could not go out, but that I could come to her home and help her babysit her younger brother. I was convinced this meant that we were going to have a really hot date. I was ecstatic. When the night of the date arrived, I went to her house only to discover that several of her other friends were there as well. This was a mild letdown for me, but a little later when her boyfriend also came to visit, I was devastated. Trying to be part of the school's social life generated many intense feelings and emotions in me.

SPECIAL EDUCATION TO THE RESCUE

A critical part of my experience in public school was having access to a special education teacher who was trained to work with visually impaired students. Mrs. Landis traveled to the five or six public schools in her area. She met with me once a week and discussed any problems I was having. When I was having difficulty with particular teachers, she would help them understand how to be most effective in working with a sightless student. In addition, she would spend time helping me solve problems related to various social challenges I was encountering.

In the tenth grade I took first-year German, and the teacher had almost no concept of what it meant to work with blind students; he probably did not feel that he should have to teach someone without sight. He asked an older student to read my exam to me, and because the student had mistakenly misread the instructions, I failed. The teacher refused to believe that such a mistake had occurred, and, consequently, he would not change my grade. He also would make comments in class about how I had not learned the material properly and that I needed to study harder. Mrs. Landis, the special education teacher, helped me work out this difficult situation. The school later fired that German teacher.

A TEACHER LEARNS A LESSON

In my junior year I took physics, and I recall that my relationship with this teacher began in an interesting way. On the first day of school, I entered her class before she came into the room; therefore, she did not see me stumbling to my seat. As the class began, she started by discussing the physical concept of gravity. When I raised my hand with a question about her explanation, she answered by drawing an instructive diagram on the blackboard. I felt right away that I would be in deep trouble if she responded to my inquiries with diagrams. Next, she asked me a question about the drawing. I explained in front of the whole class that I was blind and could not see what she had drawn. When she told me to get glasses, the students who had known me for several years started to laugh.

Next, she moved on and began distributing textbooks for the class. At the end of the period, she asked us all to read the first chapter in the book. Since I was unable to read the text in front of me, I simply sat quietly in my desk. Perceiving me as lazy and unwilling to do the assignment, she confronted me in front of the class: "Why," she asked, "are you not reading the first chapter?" I responded by explaining, once again, that I was blind. Again, she did not seem to believe me. After the class was over, another teacher explained to her that I was not being a wiseguy, but that I was, simply, without sight. She was understandably upset and found me outside after school to apologize for the misunderstanding. However, it was clear that she would have a lot of trouble appreciating my special needs.

After doing well in her class for the first half of the year, I started the second half with a conflict. She was very upset because I was not having my tests timed, and she perceived this to be an unfair advantage. So, she started to time my exams. Obviously, she could not know how much more time I would need, thus the time she allotted was little more than a guess. I felt that this was extremely unfair. I gained a great deal of support from Mrs. Landis, who listened to my frustration with a very patient ear. However, she could not change the teacher's mind and I was forced to do the best I could. Initially, I became very depressed and developed an attitude that I just didn't care. However, after doing poorly on several subsequent tests, I started feeling very angry. As my anger developed, I started to understand that the teacher was winning and that I was proving her point by not performing well. Mrs. Landis helped me to channel my anger so that I could use this frustrating situation to motivate myself to study more intensely. In the midst of my anger, I came to realize that in order to prove my teacher wrong I had to work harder. This realization sparked my campaign to embarrass the teacher and show her that I was the best darned student she had and, more importantly, that she was treating me unfairly.

Consequently, I began studying physics with a renewed determination. I felt that I had become one with the subject, since I stayed up until 3:00 a.m. to learn physics like I had never learned anything else before. My anger became my best friend, motivating me to excel. When the time came for the final exam, I was ready. The teacher told me I would have twice the time the other students had and that Mrs. Landis would read the test to me. I still remember that day and recall how quickly the exam went by. I was stunned to discover that I had completed the test with plenty of time left over. Several days later, the teacher came to me and apologized, saying that I had achieved the second-highest grade in the class; I received an A in the course. Several weeks later, when I took the physics college entrance examination, I was surprised to learn that I had scored an 800 on this test, the highest score possible.

This experience demonstrated to me that I could use my anger to move forward instead of letting it block me from my goals. Too often I have seen angry people giving up and allowing anger to destroy their lives rather than propel them to higher levels of accomplishment.

TRACKING FOR BETTER AND FOR WORSE

When I entered the public school system, administrators wrestled with the question of which roster, or level of academia, I should be placed in. Their final decision was to put me in the middle rosters so that I would not be overwhelmed with academic pressure. After I did well my first year in the sighted school, the administrator cautiously moved me to a science class in an academically talented roster. After performing well in my classes (including the honors class) during my second year in public school, I was placed in the academically talented science class, but in the middle roster for all other classes, including English, history, and math. When I graduated several years later, I had maintained a very good grade point average, but wasn't given the chance to benefit from the extra credit I might have obtained had I been placed in the honors classes.

My senior year, I only applied to two colleges, both of them very competitive. Since I had performed well in my classes, I expected to be accepted by at least one of the two schools. In fact, I often stayed up nights during my final year worrying about which school I would attend if both schools accepted me. In April, I was shocked to learn that neither school had accepted me, and so I began wondering if I should return to high school for one more year. I often think that if I had been pushed a little more in high school, and if I had been given the opportunity to take the honors classes, I might not have been rejected from both of those colleges.

I realized, too, that I should have applied to other highly competitive schools in order to increase my chances of being accepted by one of them.

What really happened, however, may have been the best thing that could have occurred. At the last minute, I was accepted by Gettysburg College, the same school that my parents had attended. Gettysburg allowed me to apply late in the spring of my senior year, and they accepted me. This small college turned out to be the best fit for me. The professors were wonderful, and they gave me an opportunity to excel. In spite of the fact that everything worked out for the best, I do recommend that students with disabilities be challenged in their schoolwork. Students who are performing well should be placed in honors programs to allow them the same opportunities as other able students. I do not fault my high school for being cautious initially, but I do feel that they might have moved me to the honors classes once I had proven myself.

ENVISIONING THE DREAM

Around eighth or ninth grade, I developed my crazy dream of becoming a physician. I began to explore the idea with friends and family. Most of them thought that I had lost my mind. Although my parents seemed to think that it was an idea worth exploring, they were skeptical. I remember talking to a psychiatrist about the possibility, and he told me that sight was not important in the practice of his work, but that there was no way a blind student could navigate medical school. I also learned that there were psychiatrists who were blind, but they had gone through their training with sight and had lost their vision after graduating from medical school.

I discussed the idea of becoming a physician with some of my high school teachers, and in one case, a teacher had a special meeting with my parents to express his concerns that I had not developed a realistic plan for my future. It was important, he told them, to help me create a more practical plan for my vocational goals. He felt it was his role to instruct my parents to guide me into more realistic dreams.

In my junior year of high school, my parents and I decided to go right to the "horse's mouth" and talk to the director of admissions at the University of Pennsylvania. I recall receiving a letter from a Dr. K., saying that he would take the time to talk to me and discuss the idea of a blind student attending medical school at the university. To me, that letter meant that he was obviously interested in the plan. When my mother and I arrived to meet with him, we were extremely anxious. The dean spoke with us for 45 minutes, and throughout the meeting he said again and again how unrealistic the whole idea was. I needed, he advised, to develop more practical goals for my future. I was devastated, but my mother was convinced that the dean was right. Naturally, when you tell an adolescent that he cannot do something, he becomes even more determined to do it. That's exactly how I felt about pursuing my dream. While I was upset with the meeting, I was even more determined to become a doctor someday.

This story of my visit to the dean has an interesting ending. Later, after finishing my classes in medical school, I had to take an examination called the National Boards in order to receive a license. A medical degree is worthless if one can't pass the National Boards and be licensed to practice medicine. Since the exam had to be read to me, special authorization was required to take the test in this fashion, and I had to write a letter to the head of the National Boards to request permission. As luck would have it, the doctor to whom I had to write was the same person I had talked to in my junior year of high school. He turned out to be a wonderful man, who arranged to have the test read to me, and at the end of his letter he wrote, "I am glad you did not take my advice."

INSIGHTS

From the high school experience of being a sightless student in a sighted world, I learned that the most powerful lessons are not always in the books; that sighted teachers and students need to be educated about how sightless students struggle to achieve in their world and how much they want to be a natural part of that world; and that sightless students need a strong family and special educators, advocates like Mrs. Landis. Most of all, I learned that they need a dream, the encouragement to pursue it, and the determination to achieve it. Although others thought that my dream of becoming a physician was unrealistic, I had a vision, and I have seen that vision become my reality.

Extracurricular Activities and Students with Disabilities

Cynthia Ann Bowman

REQUIRED COURSES AND ELECTIVES

Lesley has a cognitive impairment that sometimes causes her to have trouble with instructions. Learning new games or activities in physical education (PE) can be very hard for her to do quickly. Lesley found that she often did not know what to do when they had a new sport or activity in class. The PE teachers saw that this was a problem and gave her two choices: either her Individualized Education Program (IEP) could be redone so that she did not have to take PE classes, or they could devise alternate activities that she could do during these course periods. Lesley liked to exercise and wanted to continue taking PE, so she asked that they try the second option. Whenever she got confused by the instructions for the day's recreation, the PE teachers told her to do an activity in the gym that she could do safely on her own. They agreed that she could use the weight room or run on the indoor track on her own without its being a safety problem. This agreement turned PE from a frustration to one of Lesley's favorite classes.

It is important to have opportunities to participate in activities you enjoy; without such experiences, school can quickly become a tedious task rather than an avenue for exploration. Therefore, if a required course or elective has moments when your disability becomes an issue, talk to your teachers, guidance counselor, or school administrators about modifications that reveal your strengths and fulfill your needs.

DON'T LET ACCESS BE A BARRIER

Sally, a wheelchair user, started classes at her new high school and found she had a problem. She could get around most of the rooms and hallways on campus without a problem, but the doorway to the computer lab had a frame that she could not get her chair over by herself. When she approached the school administration about the problem and showed the principal how difficult the doorway was for her, the school had the problem corrected. Sally was very pleased with the results, and several other students who had mobility impairments thanked her for making it easier for them to get into the computer lab. Because of this experience, Sally formed a schoolwide organization for students with disabilities to discuss issues they were facing and, when appropriate, to bring those issues to the attention of the administration. Sally turned an obstacle into a way to make herself and her fellow students with disabilities advocates for their own rights at school.

Students with physical disabilities often have mobility difficulties in many areas of school and extracurricular activities. Football games in local/school stadiums, basketball games in crowded gymnasiums, tight space in newspaper and/or yearbook rooms, and crowded hallways and lockers can add to a student's frustration. So much of high school is social and revolves around extracurricular activities. Finding your niche in such activities can make a huge difference in your sense of belonging. You may have to seek help with access if you participate or attend athletic events, including:

- Football games
- Basketball games
- Swim meets
- Wrestling matches
- Baseball games
- Soccer games
- Tennis and golf matches

Sports, however, are not the only extracurricular activities. For those students who enjoy the arts, there a myriad of activities, including:

- Band
- Chorus
- Glee Club
- Spirit Band
- Drama
- Literary Magazine
- Yearbook
- Newspaper

For students who prefer more academic activities, there are always:

- National Honor Society
- Student Government
- Chess Club
- Brain Bowls
- French Club
- Spanish Club
- Academic Olympics

Many schools also have service organizations, including:

- Key Club
- Kiwanis, Rotary, and other student affiliates
- 4-H
- Future Farmers, Teachers, Lawyers, Doctors, etc.
- Environmental Activist Groups
- Political Organizations
- Scouting

In addition to clubs, athletics, music, and art, there are always a variety of school-sponsored events, such as:

- Pep Rallies
- Dances
- Homecoming Parades, Bonfires
- Spirit Days
- Guest Speakers
- Academic Fairs
- Class Meetings
- Fund-raising
- Intramural Sports and Activities

By participating in activities you enjoy, others will see the real you and soon forget your disability. Not only do you develop skills for beyond school, but you also take an active role in school life, making friends and sharing talents.

Max, for example, is a talented student who is adept at a number of subjects and his favorite class is math, which he takes at very advanced levels. He was chosen to be a part of the school's competitive math team, which participates in tournaments against other schools in the district and the state. Being asked to join the team was a major honor for two reasons: first, everyone else on the team was in a higher grade than Max, and second, it took Max a little longer to do the problems than other students because his sight was not very good. But the fact that he did math problems so well made him an ideal choice for the math team.

Max was excited to go to his first tournament. As the general instructions were being given to the teams, it became clear that many of the problems in the competition would be displayed to the entire room on a projection screen. This would not be a problem when the team members were working together. However, for the individual problems, Max would not be able to read the screen. He mentioned this to the faculty sponsor, who apologized for not thinking to ask in advance about the setup to make certain there would be no problems. Max had not thought to ask, since he had never been to one of these tournaments before and did not know how it would be set up. Fortunately, the sponsor was able to talk to the judges in time, and Max was given a written version of each problem for the individual competition. And he did very well for his team.

Every student comes to the classroom with a unique set of characteristics, talents, and beliefs that cannot always be scientifically analyzed. As human beings, we are all complex and the nature of this complexity is why we can achieve our goals. Creating value and meaning in everything within and outside of the classroom will open up the possibilities for students to grow and begin their journey of continuous transformation.

Dating Considerations for Adolescents with Disabilities

Phyllis A. Gordon and Molly K. Tschopp

As an individual moves through adolescence, he or she frequently encounters a range and intensity of emotions, both old and new. Young people may experience numerous feelings—such as excitement, fear, self-doubt, challenge, and happiness—which can occur simultaneously and become even more confusing. Though adolescents often hear from parents and teachers that this confusion is normal, it usually doesn't feel so normal when it is happening to you. One particular area that can create many questions and concerns for most young people is the development of interpersonal relationships, specifically as they relate to dating and intimacy issues. For adolescents with disabilities, these concerns may be even more heightened because they may have limited opportunities to develop dating skills or even to think of themselves as potential dating partners. This may be due to both the characteristics of their disability and/or illness and the messages received from others (e.g., parents, teachers, peers) that exclude the notion of dating and sexuality for persons with disabilities.

Adolescence is a time of immense change and self-discovery. According to Bramble (1995), it is a period when young people typically become focused on themselves and their bodies. While this is normal for all adolescents, it may be a particularly difficult time for those with disabilities because of fears and/or concerns that they do not match the standards society requires in terms of physique and abilities. Some adolescents with disorders such as cerebral palsy or muscular dystrophy may have bodies that do not always act as intended (Taleporos & McCabe, 2001). Some disabilities may cause spasticity and mobility difficulties; others may create communication disorders. Although fears about body image may be exacerbated for those with disabilities, nearly all teenagers experience concern about some aspect of their bodies or abilities. This has even been identified by some researchers as the "myth of bodily perfection," which really suggests that few people live up to the images portrayed on television and in movies (Stone, 1995).

Fortunately, current research has begun to identify that the need for close and romantic relationships as well as for dating opportunities is equally as important for those with disabilities as for the nondisabled. In addition, it is well known that dating and disability are not incongruent concepts. This discussion focuses on several areas related to issues of dating and relationship development for adolescents with disabilities, such as friendship building, interpersonal communication, and self-esteem. Issues related to successful dating are identified, and a list of resources available is provided for those with further interest in the topic.

FRIENDSHIP DEVELOPMENT

Being friends and having friends are important components to positive adjustment and identity development. In making the transition to high school, adolescents are often confronted with finding their place in a larger social setting where they are meeting and interacting with many new and diverse groups of people. The ability to establish and maintain friendships is important in order to diminish feelings of isolation and loneliness as well as create a niche or crowd where one feels comfort and acceptance. It has also been suggested that those who believe themselves to be competent in making friends have been found less vulnerable to the challenges of adapting to a new school, and strains that may occur in peer relations as friends move to new or differing settings (Fenzel, 2000).

It is through the development of friendship that children learn to acquire interpersonal skills critical in adulthood. In fact, research has indicated that the ability to make friends is one of the best predictors of adult adaptation (Hartup, 1992). Therefore, this is an important skill for adolescents, both with and without disabilities. Friendship building is typically not different for those with disabilities (when compared to those without disabilities), but issues of disability sometimes create distinct problems that may require the development of special skills in order to navigate relationships with peers. Furthermore, good friendships are important because they provide the developmental foundation upon which romantic relationships are based (Seiffge-Krenke, 2000). Plainly speaking, many skills utilized in developing and sustaining friendships are essential in creating more intimate relationships. Consequently, for adolescents with an interest in dating, the importance of learning how to be a good friend cannot be ignored.

Friendships develop from a mutual decision between two or more individuals to associate, and involve both trust and loyalty (Green, Schleien, Mactavish & Benepe, 1995; Zajac & Hartup, 1997). The responsibilities inherent in maintaining friendships actually differ somewhat based on the age or developmental stage of individuals. While children in preschool or kindergarten will most likely select friends based on who is available, requirements for friendship change as individuals grow older. During adolescence, individuals build and maintain friendships based on factors such as feelings of support, trust, and a belief that one's friend understands and can empathize with his or her experiences (Doll, 1996). The commitments and obligations of friendship evolve and change as one grows older, and it is important that young people develop the appropriate and necessary skills as they mature. They may need to be taught the importance of specific skills, such as maintaining a friend's confidences or standing by a friend in times of trouble. These are obligations for all friends, and as one grows older, they only become more important.

There are a number of books and videos that examine the issues of friendship. *The Cure* (1995) is an excellent movie that reveals the poignant story of how two young, adolescent boys, one who has AIDS, become friends and how that friendship changes both of their lives. Through their relationship, they are challenged to grow and participate in life in ways they could never have imagined. In addition, Bowman and Gordon (2000) provide suggestions about books that speak to issues of adolescents with disabilities and friendship. One example is *Izzy, Willy-Nilly* (1986) written by Cynthia Voigt, a book that looks at the impact of an accidental disability on the life of a popular girl in her sophomore year of high school. In this story, Izzy faces many issues and problems related to self-image, friendships, and dating. In addition to fictional portrayals, a number of educational videos are available and provide excellent information concerning the importance of friendships.

DATING/ROMANTIC INVOLVEMENT

Many people believe that the feature most important for romantic involvement is intimacy or the ability to share personal thoughts and feelings in a close relationship (Seiffge-Krenke, 2000). Some factors that influence an adolescent's ability to date are communication and social skills, finding and attracting a partner to date, opportunities to interact, and knowledge about issues of sexuality (Kewman, Warschausky, Engel & Warzak, 1997). Each plays a part in the dating process.

INTERPERSONAL COMMUNICATION

The impact of one's disability on interpersonal communication is actually unknown. While many researchers have identified a difficulty in relationship development due to disability, the fact remains that individuals with disabilities make friends, find romantic partners, marry, and have families. Nevertheless, most people with a disabling condition have perceived discomfort in others due to their disability, have faced issues of staring or curiosity, and have had to deal with insensitive remarks or comments. All of these experiences may influence views of self and hinder the ability to see oneself in a positive manner. Obviously, people without disabilities need to be held accountable for their acceptance of and beliefs in stereotypes and myths that view those with disabilities as being different or inferior. But people with disabilities must also assume some responsibility in helping these interactions become easier.

Why is it important for a person with a disability to ease interaction difficulties, and what exactly can he or she do? Well, perhaps most importantly, by assuming responsibility in relationship development, individuals with disabilities achieve an element of control. They can take proactive steps to promote positive communication. There have been several strategies suggested to encourage interactions between those with and without disabilities. One such technique has been termed "acknowledgment of disability" (Davis, 1961). Within this strategy, the person with the disability acknowledges or casually allows the topic of his or her disability to enter the conversation. An example of this concerns one of the authors of this chapter, who has been disabled for years and uses a cane in order to walk.

Frequently when meeting new people for the first time, I mention my cane in context to a different topic such as, "before I used a cane, I loved to play tennis. Did you see the match on Saturday?" This mention of disability serves several purposes. It lets those without a disability know that I am comfortable with myself and with speaking about my disability, and that they are free from worry or concern about hurting my feelings if they mention the cane or disability. Basically, I am giving them permission to acknowledge that they "noticed." Most importantly, though, I am letting them know that there is more to me than my cane. I love tennis, which can be a beginning foundation for further conversation.

There have been other suggestions about ways to influence interactions and communication more positively. Not surprisingly, many people both with and without disabilities sometimes feel uncomfortable with their abilities to be socially successful. Most adolescents (as well as many adults) have an unrealistic concern about their social skills. Some individuals feel shy or nervous when meeting new people, and some worry about the adequacy of their skills (e.g., Will I say the right thing? What if I say something that makes me look foolish?). There are a few things that might be helpful for those who find themselves becoming easily nervous or anxious during social interactions.

First, it might be beneficial to meet with a school or community counselor to discuss these concerns. Counselors are trained and work continually with young people who are experiencing lowered self-esteem and problems in handling social situations. A counselor can assist in developing an understanding of both the source of the problem areas and their remedy. In many cases, disability will not be the focal point. Even for most adolescents who don't have a disability, social concerns are fairly common. A counselor helps individuals to gain skills for better communication, even suggesting at times a group counseling situation where adolescents can discuss their thoughts and concerns with others experiencing similar difficulties. These groups will generally include both disabled and nondisabled persons, and the goal is to help individuals become comfortable with themselves and others in social settings.

Another method that can help in the development of good social skills is to role-play and practice ways to handle simulated situations (Bandura, 1977). Rehearsal and practice allow advance preparation of the responses that you might make in any anticipated situation. For example, many adolescents practice (either alone or "on a friend") the skill of asking a friend out on a date. When rehearsing with another, the practice partner can respond in several different ways (e.g., yes, no, I'll think about it) in order to prepare for any eventual response, so that one feels confident about handling the situation. An additional approach may be to observe another student who you feel is very confident in social situations and begin to emulate some of his or her behaviors. This does not mean changing who you are to copy the behavior, but to use those observed behaviors as a model to better improve your own skills.

Finally, there are also a number of excellent videos that focus on disability presentation and the differing ways people react to their disabling condition. The video *As I Am* (1990) shows three young people with developmental disabilities talking about their lives, hopes, and goals. It highlights the similarities between those with and without disabilities. Another excellent video, *Without Pity* (1997), is narrated by Christopher Reeve and looks at the lives and experiences of several people living with disabilities. Included in the film is a young boy without arms and legs, who describes his interactions with his regular education classroom peers. The video also describes the impact of an accident on a young high school age male and the struggles he goes through in order to rebuild his life and relationships.

ATTRACTING A PARTNER

Dating is an age-appropriate task for most adolescents (Seiffge-Krenke, 2000). Physical and emotional attraction to others is a normal part of human development. Although the majority of people are attracted to the opposite sex, about 10 percent of the general population is attracted to persons of the same sex. This is most likely similar in the disabled population.

Finding and attracting a partner has been difficult for people with disabilities to some extent, particularly for those who are young. It appears that these individuals more often begin dating at a later age, but this does not seem to occur due to lack of interest (Rousso, 1996). Often it results from the lack of opportunity, feelings of low self-esteem, and, in some cases, the attitudes of others. One of the main ways to enter the dating scene is to get actively involved in school and outside organizations. The more opportunities one has to meet other adolescents, the chances are greater that a connection will be made. Adolescents should be encouraged to participate in school-sponsored events and activities (e.g., clubs, committees) in order to develop and improve social skills and learn to interact with the opposite sex in nonthreatening settings. Additional activities might be to get involved in church or service learning projects. Involvement in activities that benefit others also provides one with a sense of competence and confidence (Scales, Blythe, Berkas & Kielsmeier, 2000). These traits are attractive to others and help build self-esteem. Adolescents also learn about dating from their friends. Some research suggests that friends actually have the most influence on adolescents' dating choices (Wood, Senn, Desmarais, Park & Verberg, 2002). Access to peer activities is important because informal education about dating and sexuality (e.g., sexual knowledge, attitudes) is often gained through these interactions.

SELF-ESTEEM ISSUES

The feelings one holds about him or herself are really the key. Self-esteem refers, in part, to the picture we have in our minds about ourselves. Our self-image is determined not only by our physical appearance, but also includes perceptions about our abilities and skills (Bramble, 1995). Much of what we think about ourselves develops through our observation and estimation of our abilities in comparison to others. As Kewman and colleagues (1997) noted, adolescents with disabilities who only see their nondisabled peers relating intimately may begin to doubt whether it can or will be a part of their lives, too. Consequently, one critical factor necessary to improve the self and sexual image of adolescents with disabilities is to provide images that more closely reflect them. There are two videos in particular that discuss disability and issues of sexuality in an honest, forthright manner. In the video *My Body Is Not Who I Am* (1993), several young adults discuss the implications of their disabilities with regard to attitudes, relationships, dating, and sexuality. They describe several areas of importance and raise issues and questions young people might be concerned about but are uncomfortable bringing up. Another video, *Towards Intimacy* (1992), looks at the relationships between different couples when one of the partners is disabled. The participants in the film talk frankly about issues of sexuality, interpersonal relationships, and marriage.

In addition, there are several strategies to help people work on self-esteem issues. First, the more individuals believe that they can be successful (self-efficacy), the more likely they are to exhibit positive behaviors and high levels of self-esteem (Sclenker & Trudeau, 1990). Adolescents with disabilities may benefit from training, particularly in the area of assertiveness. Those who are more assertive appear to be better able to ignore negative attitudes of others and maintain positive views of self.

Another means of maintaining positive self-esteem involves enlarging one's set of values to include a variety of personal dimensions (Dembo, Leviton & Wright, 1956). Frequently, adolescents (and adults also) only think of and look at themselves in very narrow terms. Rather than perceiving themselves in totality (e.g., I am a helpful son, I am a great brother, I am a good and trusting friend, etc.), they tend to focus on specific elements, such as physique. As physical abilities are only one aspect of our personality, efforts need to be made to expand our self-observation. One video that provides a wonderful example of seeing oneself in greater terms is *Withstanding Ovation* (1994), which shows two adolescents with disabilities who have moved their lives far beyond their physical limitations in both thoughts and actions. They provide excellent role modeling in terms of relegating disability to only one portion of a person's life.

KNOWLEDGE OF SEXUALITY AND EDUCATION

All people are sexual beings and have sexual needs. Sexuality includes one's thoughts, feelings, personality, sex drive, and sexual activities. It is part of lifelong development that includes biological, psychological, social, and ethical aspects (Planned Parenthood Federation of America, Inc., 2000). While some disabilities (e.g., quadriplegia) involve a change in sexual functioning, this does not mean a loss of the emotional aspects of sexuality. Sexuality is a natural part of everyone's life that helps to define who we are and how we express ourselves to others. Misperceptions about individuals with disabilities frequently include the beliefs that they are asexual, unable to engage in sexual activity, or lack sexual desire (Asch & Fine, 1988; Boyle, 1994; DeLoach, 1994). Consequently, individuals with disabilities have often been expected to repress their sexuality and deny their rights to sexual expression (Monat-Haller, 1992). They may not receive adequate sex education either, due to these misperceptions. Delayed sexual development may be associated with this lack of knowledge about one's own sexuality and sexuality in general (Kewman et al., 1997).

SEXUAL KNOWLEDGE

Sexuality can be a difficult or uncomfortable subject to discuss. However, gaining knowledge about one's own sexuality is essential to making informed decisions and choices. This involves an exploration of one's values and attitudes toward sexuality. Problem-solving and decision-making skills related to options and the consequences of choices are also critical. Similar to their nondisabled peers, adolescents with disabilities need information about fertility, contraception, adoption, genetic counseling, pregnancy, parenting, sexually transmitted diseases, and sexual dysfunction. In addition, they need information related to differences between public and private behaviors, as well as a clear delineation of socially inappropriate sexual behaviors.

Communicating effectively, setting boundaries, and asserting oneself are essential knowledge for adolescents learning to negotiate relationships. Communication is especially important in intimate involvements, where partners are expected to share information about their thoughts, feelings, and needs. Assertiveness plays an important role in relationships and the expression of one's sexuality. Being clear with one's partner about the acceptability of physical contact and the establishment of boundaries are critical to maintaining one's self-respect and rights. Saying "no" when one is uncomfortable with a partner's actions is a right, and should be respected by both members of the relationship.

Individuals with disabilities are often vulnerable to abuse. Research has indicated that children with disabilities are maltreated 1.7 times more often than those without disabilities (Crosse, Kaye & Ratnofsky, 1992). Therefore, sex education is essential so that abuse can be prevented (Jurkowski & Amado, 1993). It is imperative that adolescents with disabilities understand their right to say no, and to report any violations they have experienced to trusted adults. Effective sex education and understanding the right to refuse sexual advances are important factors in protecting adolescents with disabilities from exploitation (Committee on Children with Disabilities, 1996) and are essential for the promotion of healthy sexual development.

RESOURCES FOR GAINING SEXUAL KNOWLEDGE

Sexual knowledge may be gained from multiple sources, including peers, family members, health-care professionals, and formal instructional materials and self-help resources. Peers provide an important resource for adolescents in the development and understanding of sexuality. Skills utilized in developing and maintaining friendships are the foundation for acquiring more intimate relationships, which may include love and physical affection. Access to socialization opportunities with peers with and without disabilities is also an important step in expelling any misperceptions about disability. The importance of the role that peers play in gaining sexual knowledge is demonstrated in the development and use of such formal sex education programs as the Planned Parenthood Federation of America Peer Education Programs for Teens (2002).

Families are also integral in the early sex education of adolescents with disabilities, particularly in terms of transmitting family values. However, many parents may have little knowledge about sexuality and disability issues, or may be uncomfortable discussing sexuality issues with their children. It is important for parents and family members to understand that adolescents with disabilities need information, social opportunities, and privacy just as much as other young people. They need to communicate with their family members openly and honestly about both familial values and their developing interest in areas of sexuality. Often, health-care providers can assist adolescents and parents in finding ways to begin communicating about these issues.

Sexuality education is important in enhancing quality of life and the development of a mutually satisfying relationship. Adolescents with disabilities and their partners may have questions and concerns about how a disability will affect social and sexual activities. How one's body moves, limitations in movement due to disability, or any pain associated with physical contact may be important topics to address. Discussing how a disability may affect such activities may be difficult at first, but it is important in establishing an open line of communication in the relationship. It is often helpful for adolescents to think in advance about how they might discuss their disability or respond to questions about sex and disability. Practicing these responses with a trusted friend or role-playing with a parent or counselor can provide added confidence when these topics arise.

Health-care professionals such as physicians, nurses, and health secretaries can assist adolescents with disabilities in learning more about healthy sexual behaviors, such as exploring birth control options and using precautions to avoid acquisition and spread of sexually transmitted diseases. Educators and counselors can also help adolescents in learning techniques to avoid sexual exploitation, identifying moral and emotional aspects of sexuality, and understanding how societal attitudes toward disability and sexuality affect adolescents with disabilities. Along with individual counseling and instruction, health-care providers often use structured skill-training programs for groups, such as those published by James Stanfield, which are aimed at improving understanding of sexuality and relationships.

CONCLUSION

Adolescents can also access various self-help resources such as online Web sites, books, and relevant videos. Online resources focused on providing sexuality and relationship information for adolescents include such sites as TeenWire (http://www.teenwire.com) sponsored by the Planned Parenthood Federation of America, and TeensHealth (http://www.teenshealth.org) sponsored by the Nemours Foundation. TeensHealth is focused on improving the health and spirit of young people and provides numerous health-related topics, including sexual health. The home page of the National Information Center for Children and Youth with Disabilities (NICHCY), located at http://www.nichcy.org, is a national information and referral center for information on disability and disability-related issues relevant to adolescents. In addition, a resource list for programs and videos is provided below.

SEX EDUCATION AND RELATIONSHIPS PROGRAMS

Becoming DateSmart-1: Abstinence and the Art of Saying "No"

This video program provides junior and senior high school students with information about the choice of abstinence and how to set sexual boundaries (available at http://www.stanfield.com/sexed.html).

Becoming DateSmart-2: Avoiding Trouble and Listening for "No"

This video program provides junior and senior high school students with information about how to refrain from sexually exploitive behaviors (available at http://www.stanfield.com/sexed.html).

Circles I: Intimacy and Relationships

A well-known and widely used video program by Leslie Walker-Hirsch, MED, and Marklyn P. Champagne, RN, MSW, aimed at teaching students with disabilities about social distance and relationship building (available at http://www.stanfield.com/sexed.html).

Circles II: Stop Abuse

A video program by Leslie Walker-Hirsch, MED, and Marklyn P. Champagne, RN, MSW, focused on teaching students how to recognize and avoid sexually exploitive situations (available at http://www.stanfield.com/sexed.html).

Life Horizons I: The Physiological and Emotional Aspects of Being Male and Female

A widely used sex education program for individuals with developmental and learning disabilities. This slide program includes such topic areas as parts of the body, sexual life cycle, human reproduction, birth control or regulation of fertility, and more (available at http://www.stanfield.com/sexed.html).

Life Horizons II: The Moral, Social, and Legal Aspects of Sexuality

This educational slide program provides material on the psychosocial aspects of sexuality. It includes such topics as self-esteem; moral, legal, and social aspects; and dating skills (available at http://www.stanfield.com/sexed.html).

Life Facts: Teacher-Friendly Life Skills Program Series

This series consists of seven programs that include material on basic sex education, self-protection skills, AIDS, managing emotions, skills to avoid exploitation, substance abuse, and managing illness and injury (available at http://www.stanfield.com/sexed.html).

GENERAL VIDEOS

Brodie, J. (1990). *As I Am.* VHS. Boston, MA: Fanlight Productions.
The Cure. (1995). VHS. MCA Home Video.
McGee, D. & Hubert, N. (1992). *Toward Intimacy.* VHS. New York: Filmmakers Library.
Mierendorf, M. (1997). *Without Pity.* VHS. Princeton, NJ: Films for the Humanities and Sciences.
My Body Is Not Who I Am. (1993). VHS. Sherborn, MA: Aquarius Productions.
Texas Scottish Rite Hospital for Children. (1994). *Withstanding Ovation.* VHS. Boston, MA: Fanlight Productions.

REFERENCES

Asch, A. & Fine, M. (1988). Introduction: Beyond pedestals. In M. Fine & A. Asch (Eds.), *Women with disabilities: Essays in psychology, culture, and politics* (pp. 1–37). Philadelphia, PA: Temple University Press.
Bandura, A. (1977). Self-efficacy: Toward a unifying theory of behavioral change. *Psychological Review, 84,* 191–215.
Bowman, C.A. & Gordon, P.A. (2000). Izzy, Willy-Nilly: Issues of disability for adolescents and their families. In C.A. Bowman (Ed.), *Using literature to help troubled teenagers cope with health issues* (pp. 27–50). Westport, CT: Greenwood Press.
Boyle, P.S. (1994). Rehabilitation counselors as providers: The issue of sexuality. *Journal of Applied Rehabilitation Counseling, 25,* 6–9.
Bramble, K. (1995). Body image. In I.M. Lubkin (Ed.), *Chronic illness: Impact and interventions* (3rd ed.) (pp. 285–299). Boston, MA: Jones and Bartlett Publishers.
Committee on Children with Disabilities. (1996). Sexuality education of children and adolescents with developmental disabilities. *Pediatrics, 97*(2), 275–278.
Crosse, S.B., Kaye, E. & Ratnofsky, A.C. (1992). *A report on the maltreatment of children with disabilities.* Washington, DC: National Center on Child Abuse and

Neglect, Administration on Children, Youth and Families, Administration for Children and Families, U.S. Department of Health and Human Services.

Davis, F. (1961). Deviance disavowal: The management of strained interaction by the visibly handicapped. *Social Problems, 9*, 120–132.

DeLoach, C.P. (1994). Attitudes toward disability: Impact on sexual development and forging of intimate relationships. *Journal of Applied Rehabilitation Counseling, 25*, 18–25.

Dembo, T., Leviton, G.L. & Wright, B.A. (1956). Adjustment to misfortune: A problem of social-psychological rehabilitation. *Artificial Limbs, 3*(2), 4.62.

Doll, B. (1996). Children without friends: Implications for practice and policy. *Social Psychology Review, 25*, 165–183.

Fenzel, L.M. (2000). Prospective study of changes in global self-worth and strain during the transition to middle school. *Journal of Early Adolescence, 20*, 93–116.

Green, F.P., Schleien, S.J., Mactavish, J. & Benepe, S. (1995). Nondisabled adults' perceptions of relationships in the early stages of arranged partnerships with peers with mental retardation. *Educational and Training in Mental Retardation and Developmental Disabilities, 30*(2), 91–108.

Hartup, W.W. (1992). *Having friends, making friends, and keeping friends: Relationships as educational contexts* (pp. 1–4). ERIC Digest, http://www.ericae.net/edo/ED345854.htm.

Jurkowski, E. & Amado, A.N. (1993). Affection, love, intimacy, and sexual relationships. In A.N. Amado (Ed.), *Friendships and community connections between people with and without developmental disabilities* (pp. 129–151). Baltimore, MD: Paul H. Brookes Publishing Co.

Kewman, D., Warschausky, S., Engel, L. & Warzak, W. (1997). Sexual development of children and adolescents. In M.L. Sipski and C.J. Alexnader (Eds.), *Sexual function in people with disabilities and chronic illness: A health professional's guide* (pp. 355–378). Gaithersburg, MD: Aspen Publishers, Inc.

Monat-Haller, R.K. (1992). *Understanding and expressing sexuality: Responsible choices for individuals with developmental disabilities.* Baltimore, MD: Paul H. Brookes Publishing Co.

Planned Parenthood Federation of America, Inc. (2000). *Choosing a sexuality education curriculum.* Retrieved March 9, 2003, from http://www.plannedparenthood.org/.

———. (2002). *A guide to peer education programs for teens.* Retrieved March 9, 2003, from http://www.plannedparenthood.org/education/020808_peereducationguide.pd.

Rousso, H. (1996). Sexuality and a positive sense of self. In D.M. Krotoski, M.A. Nosek, & M.A. Turk (Eds.), *Women with physical disabilities: Achieving and maintaining health and well-being* (pp. 109–116). Baltimore, MD: Paul H. Brookes Publishing Co.

Scales, P.C., Blyth, D.A., Berkas, T.H. & Kielsmeier, J.C. (2000). The effects of service-learning on middle school students' social responsibility and academic success. *Journal of Early Adolescence, 20*, 332–358.

Sclenker, B.R. & Trudeau, J.V. (1990). Impact of self-presentations on private self-beliefs: Effects of prior self-beliefs and misattributions. *Journal of Personality and Social Psychology, 52*, 22–32.

Seiffge-Krenke, I. (2000). Diversity in romantic relations of adolescents with vary-
    ing health status: Links to intimacy in close friendships. *Journal of Adoles-
    cent Research, 15,* 611–636.
Stone, S.D. (1995). The myth of bodily perfection. *Disability and Society, 10,*
    413–424.
Taleporos, G. & McCabe, M.P. (2001). The impact of physical disability on body
    esteem. *Sexuality and Disability, 19,* 293–308.
Wood, E., Senn, C.Y., Desmarais, S., Park, L. & Verberg, N. (2002). Sources of in-
    formation about dating and their perceived influence on adolescents.
    Journal of Adolescent Research, 17, 401–417.
Zajac, R.J., & Hartup, W.W. (1997). Friends as coworkers: Research review and
    classroom implications. *Child Development, 65,* 1764–1777.

SECTION IV

Academic Issues

INTRODUCTION

This section discusses the many issues related to academic success in high school for students with disabilities. Examined in detail are strategies for success in the classroom, in the library, in studying and doing research, in using adaptive technologies and educational supports, and in writing papers. A disability cannot be allowed to prevent an individual from accomplishing personal goals; however, it definitely can shape how he or she goes about achieving those goals. Having a disability can impact the courses that students take while in high school, how they approach doing their work for their courses, and the activities they decide to participate in. Discussed in this section are reasons for making certain academic choices, the potential effects of those choices, and the strategies to succeed in fulfilling them.

The first chapter describes how to make a successful transition from middle school to high school. The following chapters discuss in detail becoming a self-advocate, using accommodations, and learning strategies for academic success. Offering particular strategies to help facilitate success, this section provides ideas on how students with disabilities can have academic and personal achievements in their classes. Also addressed are issues related to participating in classroom activities, achieving high grades in class work, conducting efficient and effective research in the library and online, writing successful papers, and participating in extracurricular activities. A specific set of study habits and tactics are offered that are tailored to the unique needs of high school students with disabilities.

Though having a disability may impact many different aspects of an individual's life, it does not have to prevent him or her from being active and successful academically. The chapters in this section can help a student with a disability achieve success in the classroom and in all other activities in which he or she is involved.

The subtitle of this section's final chapter specifies that it is aimed at educators, but it really is for everyone. Because it has been written in the language of teachers to discuss classroom issues related to educating students with disabilities, this particular chapter will be of great interest to all educators who read this book. However, it will also help students with disabilities and their parents understand how teachers conceive of curriculum issues related to disability, and it can serve as a resource that they can all share to help them better understand disability issues.

Volunteering to Rediscover Myself

High School Junior

Born 14 weeks premature, weighing in at two pounds, I was presented with my first and greatest challenge. Underdeveloped lungs and oxygen deprivation affected the use of my legs, took away my balance, stunted my growth, impeded the strength of my left hand, and affected my eyes with a condition called strabismus (where the eye muscles work independently of each other so it looks as though you're constantly cross-eyed, even though you can see normally).

Cerebral palsy has served as my single, most influential teacher—tutoring me every minute of my life. It has treated me to a lifetime of orthopedic surgeries, physical therapy, and a hard time making friends up until high school, where everyone just looked, ignored, or used me to play with my crutches (transforming them into machine guns and the like). When it all comes down to it, people don't want to look, stare, use, or be prejudiced toward anyone; they just want to understand. In turn, I wanted to understand them, to know what "normal" felt like. We all have a natural curiosity to make sense out of things, and sometimes that's the only way we can express it! I'm thankful for my cerebral palsy in so many ways . . . I'm grateful that it was from birth instead of from an accident or something, where then every day would be a struggle of comparing two different lifestyles. I'm just explaining that some good can come out of being this way . . . instead of letting it take over your life. I've been at both extremes—between feeling worthless and feeling almost too confident—and neither one is paradise.

My disability never presented problems with my self-esteem until I entered grade school, where the other kids met me with fear and indifference, and my crutches and wheelchair made them feel uncomfortable. I have experienced my share of insensitive remarks and unkind gestures from a handful of ignorant people who chose to elevate themselves at my expense. I figured out one day, however, that if I forced a smile, most of my classmates would return my glance. I needed to find a way to melt their indifference. My parents always told me that although people find it hard to look beyond the physical, sometimes your best friends are those rare people who can see the real you underneath.

It has taken me forever to come to terms with who I am as a person with cerebral palsy, and to wrap my life around it. Before, it wrapped itself around me, and I was so limited by it. I am now open to questions about my disability, which I used to find irritating. One of the goals I have set for my life has been to try to give back all of the gifts that have been given to me and to recognize those things with which I have been blessed. So I volunteer a lot. It makes me excited about little things again. Also, in my spare time, I do things I enjoy, like listening to music, sleeping, playing both guitar and piano, surfing the Internet, and reading nonrequired books.

✎ We Carved Pumpkins and Learned from Each Other ✎

Cindy

One Halloween, I shared a hospital room with Jaime, a teenager from Michigan who was diagnosed with systemic lupus eurethomyetis, more commonly known as just lupus. She had severe pain in her knees and lungs, fatigue, and a rash on her cheeks. Lupus is an autoimmune disease that affects the joints, organs, and skin. She had to see a rheumatologist and have blood tests, an EKG (electrocardiogram), and an EEG (electroencephalogram). The doctors put her on Plaquenil and Prednisone (forms of steroids). She had to take Prednisone four times a day. She wrote me later that her appearance started to change; she started to gain weight and her face got puffy. Jaime was really depressed. Her friends at school didn't know what to think, but they could tell something was happening. She did what many teens do in a crisis, just shut out many friends and classmates. Eighth grade was a hard year for Jaime because her appearance drastically changed and she fell into a pretty bad depression. In the fall of her freshman year, she was able to return to school full time. She could do everything a normal teenager can do, with the exception of being out in the sun for long periods of time.

Her family was a strong support system from the very beginning. Her dad brought pumpkins to the hospital for us to carve, and made us laugh with silly costumes and lots of candy. We both discussed how important it was to be active in school activities so other students could see our strengths and talents, and we promised to join school clubs, volunteer in the community, and attend school functions. If you or a friend has a chronic illness or is going through treatment for an illness, it's a very hard time, but having someone to talk to really helps. We shared a lot of feelings of low self-esteem and anxiety, but gave each other a greater gift of friendship and support.

Experiences of High School Students with Disabilities

Jordan has a learning disability that affects him in some classes. Though his teachers have his IEP (Individualized Education Program) and know generally about his learning disability, he has found that it really is beneficial to talk to his new teachers individually at the beginning of the school year. He tells each teacher in detail about his disability, how it affects him in class, and the ways he has found that help him to work better, in class and at home. He discusses with each of his teachers what they think would be a good strategy for applying his IEP and meeting his needs in each particular class. By being his own advocate, Jordan improves his ability to achieve in school.

Natalina's dyslexia has always made reading things on the board difficult. Her teachers know that they need to say everything they write on the board, but sometimes they forget. Natalina has learned that, if she simply reminds teachers of her needs, there is no problem. This year, however, she has a teacher who does not seem to care. She reminded the teacher, but the teacher ignored her requests, and missing what was on the board hurt Natalina's first-quarter grade in the class. She told her parents about the problem, and they asked to have a parent-teacher conference with this teacher. At the conference, her parents carefully explained Natalina's difficulties and how the teacher's actions were preventing her from doing as well as she could in the class. The conference had an impact on the teacher, who paid much better attention to Natalina's needs. Natalina vowed that, if she ever had a similar problem again, she would seek her parents' help much sooner.

Alison has Asperger's syndrome, which makes it very hard to focus on some topics in school. When she is really interested in something, she can stay focused for hours, but if a topic is hard for her to follow, she can only focus on it for a few minutes before her brain simply will not let her concentrate. One of her teachers had a very helpful idea—she asked Alison what her favorite topics were. At the start of every new topic in class, the teacher would explain how one of the things that really interested Alison related to the new topic. Alison could then follow how the ideas related, making it easier for her to focus on the new topic in class.

Maria has trouble seeing, but she does not allow it to impede her progress down the school hallways or through the rooms where her classes are held. Each year, right before school starts, she gets permission from the principal to come onto campus early. One of her teachers helps her become familiar with each room where she will be taking classes, the best walkways between her classes, and other important rooms in the area, such as the bathroom. With the teacher's assistance, Maria practices walking through new rooms and routes, familiarizing herself with navigating through her daily routine for the coming year. Taking the time to do this minimizes the problems she has getting between classes and keeps her from being late to class or getting lost early in the school year. Without these potential problems to worry about, she can concentrate on her new classes, her friends, and the activities she enjoys at school.

Bill has Tourette's syndrome, which sometimes causes him to involuntarily say things. He can't stop it, and he feels bad interrupting class when it happens. Though his teachers have handled the situation well, Bill offered them a suggestion. He proposed that there always be a desk in the hallway just outside the classroom door that he could go to when he felt an episode beginning. He could sit there until the episode passed, and that way, he would not feel like he was disrupting his classes. With the desk right outside the classroom door, his teachers could easily see how he was doing when they felt concerned.

Moving On: Ideas for You to Make Your Transition to High School Great!

Allison P. Dickey

INTRODUCTION

This chapter is written for you, the student who is "moving on" from middle school to high school. As your first day of high school approaches, you will be experiencing many thoughts and feelings that are bubbling to the surface; don't worry, those emotions are normal! After all, moving to high school is a new occurrence and you may feel a bit overwhelmed. At first glance, a high school campus can look HUGE! From your perspective, it might seem as though the buildings are bigger, the school campus is larger, and even the students are taller. To some degree your observations may be true, but even with these differences, you should not worry because you are about to begin your own high school adventure. This chapter is designed to provide you with a few helpful hints that will help make your transition to the high school experience as smooth as possible.

WHAT IS TRANSITION?

The term transition seems simple, but when it is used in a context with students with disabilities, it encompasses complex concepts (Nuehring & Sitlington, 2003). One definition of transition found in *Webster's Dictionary* (1993) is, "a passage or movement from one state, condition or place to another." In some ways, that is exactly what you are doing—moving from middle school to high school. Another definition of transition, within the Individuals with Disabilities Education Act (IDEA) of 1990 and 1997 amendments, refers to a coordinated set of activities for a student with a disability that:

a. Is designed within an outcome-oriented process, that promotes movement from school to post-secondary education, adult services, independent living or community participation; and
b. Is based on the individual student's needs, taking into account the student's preferences and interests (34 C.F.R. § 300.27).

In other words, transition is a process through which the Individualized Education Program (IEP) team can help prepare and support you for life after high school.

As stated in the federal law, the IEP team must begin to address transition issues by the age of 14, unless it is appropriate to do so earlier. These issues can include instruction, community experience, employment, postschool adult living, daily living skills, and functional vocational evaluations. In order to effectively address these areas, the IEP team wants and needs your input about your interests, thoughts, and dreams. This information is important so that your team can support your interests during high school.

This time in your life can be a very exciting and freeing experience. Remember, your input is reflective of you being an active and participating member of the IEP team. It is important for you to realize and understand that you are part of the decision-making process of planning your education. This means you have a responsibility to participate in your meetings throughout high school, not just during your eighth- or ninth-grade years. Lastly, transition planning is not a short or one-shot process; instead, your IEP and transition plan are reviewed and refined yearly during high school.

YOUR TRANSITION-PLANNING MEETING

Proactive planning has a positive effect on a typical student's adjustment to a new setting (Adreon & Stella, 2001). It is the first step in building a strong foundation for you during your transition. The second step is conducting an IEP meeting focused on your individual transition issues. Usually, before the end of your eighth-grade year or in the beginning of the ninth-grade year, the IEP team will meet to review the progress you have made on your goals and objectives from the previous year.

Transition planning involves many individuals. This team can include you, your teachers, parents/guardians, and any other stakeholders who will assist you in fulfilling your interests and dreams. It is also important to invite personnel from the high school you are going to attend to the meeting in order to coordinate your transition.

You and the IEP team will also discuss your progress in your current classes and make suggestions for classes you should enroll in during your first year of high school; this is an integral part of your transition planning. It is vital that you have successful experiences in your first year of high school. After all, during this period you begin to establish your attained credits and grade point average. These two factors can impact your future classes and class status. Once this meeting has been conducted, the IEP team should plan and follow through on the outcomes from the meeting. For instance, one outcome may be to identify the supports necessary for you to be successful in the classroom and how those services will be implemented.

As you progress through your high school years, not only will it continue to be important that you have your student supports, but you and the IEP team may begin to investigate further the options that interest you after graduation. For example, after high school you may want to attend vocational school or postsecondary (community college, college, or university) placements. If you want to live independently, you may need to meet with representatives from residential options; also, you may need to identify funding sources, and investigate other community resources that may be able to help you fulfill your goals (Nuehring & Sitlington, 2003).

Whatever you want to do after high school, these types of questions will get you thinking about your future. It will be here before you know it! Even though it seems like it will be a long time before you graduate from high school, you will be amazed at how quickly the time passes.

EXAMINING DIFFERENCES: EXPLORING THE DIFFERENCES BETWEEN MIDDLE SCHOOL AND HIGH SCHOOL

As you know, transitioning from middle school to high school can be both an exhilarating and scary time in any teenager's life. You may also be experiencing considerable physical growth and change during this time (Letrello & Miles, 2003). After all, the average teenager already feels different from everyone else! In fact, Wiles and Bondi (2002) note that middle school students, ages 10 to 14, are often characterized by emotional instability. So, with that mind-set, let's see if we can put to rest some of your concerns and explain a few basic concepts about high school. First, let's explore how high school will be different from middle school in terms of student population, campus size, classes, and graduation requirements.

The transition from middle school to high school is often associated with marked changes within the school environment (Adreon & Stella, 2001). For instance, there are often increases in school size, especially student population. This typically occurs because multiple middle schools are districted to one high school, thus increasing the total number of students. With a larger student body, the more diverse the population will become on campus. This will provide you with additional opportunities to expand your peer friendships.

Needless to say, you may feel that going from middle school to high school reminds you of when you transitioned from elementary school to middle school, and you may be right. During the move into middle school, there are two realms of student focus: concerns with being successful at schoolwork and finding new friends (Black, 1999). You may be dealing with some of the same social issues in this transition, too.

While you may still have an established circle of friends from your elementary and middle school experiences, you will have even more opportunities to make additional friends at the high school level. This is another important aspect of high school—the increased freedom of building social relationships with individuals who are your age.

You may continue to feel a sense of wanting to belong, either in a group or with a close friend, when you are in high school. One way you can meet new people is through the school's various clubs, organizations, and sports that you might find interesting. There are also parades and/or dances, like homecoming and prom, as well as other school traditions that are unique to each high school and community.

Remember, it will benefit you to participate in these activities so you can be an active member in your high school community. This is important in terms of feeling that you are "a part of" something bigger than yourself. Participating in school clubs, organizations, and/or sports can provide you with an early experience of "getting involved." High school is not just a place of learning; it is a community for living.

STUDENT ORIENTATION

Middle and high schools have varying orientation methods, the purpose of which are to familiarize you and other new students with the layout of the school campus and buildings, the academic courses and electives, and to introduce a few faculty and staff members with whom you may have regular contact at the high school (Adreon & Stella, 2001). Whatever the student orientation method may be, it is important for you to be introduced to your new environment and to be attentive during the process.

SIZE OF CAMPUS

We have briefly discussed how the size of the high school campus may be larger than what you have experienced in elementary and middle school. The school's design may not be different in terms of buildings, but they may be spread out over a larger area. Usually, high schools have buildings with two or more floors. If you have mobility issues, there will be multiple stairwells, ramps, and elevators for you to use during the school day. It would be beneficial for you to notice where you can access buildings so you can navigate the hallways in a time-effective manner.

NAVIGATING THE HALLS

Once the school day begins, at the end of each class period, you will have usually between two and six minutes to transition to your next class. On the surface, this seems like a long time, but when you are traveling from one building to another, time can elapse quickly. One thing to keep in mind is that the hallways will be filled with other students who are also trying to navigate to their next class. It would benefit you to find an effective route to travel, preferably before the school year starts; you may wish to seek assistance from school personnel and your friends to become familiar with and practice navigating the hallways beforehand. If you do not have that opportunity, you will find the best route after a few days; just try not to be tardy to your classes. If you are late, you might miss something important that is only presented at the beginning of class. The more familiar you are with the campus, the less likely you will be to get lost or be tardy.

GRADUATION REQUIREMENTS, CLASSES, AND REGISTRATION: HOW CAN I EARN A DIPLOMA?

A primary focus of secondary education is increasing the graduation rates of high school students, including those with identified disabilities. The rate at which students with disabilities fail to graduate high school is epidemic (Bakken & Kotering, 1999). Even though graduation rates and requirements have received increased emphasis, individual states have unique approaches in determining how many classes, credits, and exams are required to attain a diploma (Thurlow, Elliott, & Ysseldyke, 1998). As you enter high school, it is important that you and your family investigate and understand the options available to you as you begin to plan your curriculum. One way to start this process is for you to ask a simple question during your transition-planning meeting at the end of eighth grade, such as, "What does it take for a student with a disability to graduate from high school?"

Completing high school is considered to be an important indicator of individual student success (Lanford & Cary, 2000). In order to graduate, you may have to meet specified requirements, but these requirements can vary from state to state. It is also important for you to understand that some states may have different kinds of diplomas or certificates available to students with disabilities. For instance, Thurlow, Elliott, and Ysseldyke (1998)

note that graduation requirements can range from Carnegie unit requirements to successfully passing minimum competency tests, high school exit
exams, and/or a series of benchmarks. Additionally, requirements could
include credit, attendance, and minimum grade point average (Lanford &
Cary, 2000).

As you enroll in these classes, you will most likely have multiple teachers during the school day, each with his or her own expectations of you
and your performance during class time. With so many courses, you
must ask yourself, "How will I keep up with all my classes?" This is an
essential question to ask, and it needs to be addressed as soon as possible.
If you have organizational problems, especially in the area of keeping
track of your class work and homework, you may need to enlist the help
of your parents and teachers. The sooner you can sort out your organizational issues, the easier it will be for you to keep up in your classes.

There are other factors of student success that must also be addressed,
such as instructional expectations. You can safely assume that general education teachers have basic expectations of their students. High school can
be especially tough for students with disabilities in terms of keeping up
academically. There are common academic traits and areas of difficulty
among students with disabilities: organization, differentiating major ideas
from supporting material, comparing and contrasting, reading and understanding large amounts, relating one's background knowledge to a new set
of information, holding large quantities in memory, expressing oneself on
tests and papers, taking notes from a lecture, following verbal instructions,
working with minimum direction or feedback, and independently completing assignments over extended periods of time (Deshler et al., 2001;
Kokoszka & Drye, 1981). All of these academic factors can impact how you
perform in your classes. Students with disabilities often have difficulty in
some or all of these areas (Deshler et al., 2001; Bakken & Kotering, 2002).

If you have similar problems, then you need to be aware of your academic strengths and weaknesses so your instructional accommodations can
be tailored to your needs as a student. For instance, working with your
teachers, you could identify and learn about your preferred learning
style, as well as how to use your student supports in classes effectively.
This strategy, as well as your team-developed IEP goals and objectives,
may help you compensate in your areas of need. This leads us to our discussion of what your student special education support services look like
at the high school setting.

SUPPORT SERVICES AND FAPE

At the high school setting, the services for students with disabilities vary
at state and local levels, but one concept that does not change is FAPE (free
and appropriate public education). This means that the school district must

provide special education and related services for all students with disabil-ities at no cost to the child or her/his parents (34 C.F.R. Parts 300, 301 and Appendix C). In schools, the services for students in special education fall within a continuum of placements, which can include the following: general education class with support services, resource room, a separate class in a regular school, a separate day school, and residential settings. Your class assignments will be based on your individual student needs. This brings us to the importance of identifying, designing, and implement-ing your individual instructional accommodations.

INSTRUCTIONAL ACCOMMODATIONS

The implementation and use of instructional and classroom accommo-dations, which are sometimes called student supports, can play a vital role in academic success in your classes. In many ways, they are designed to "level the playing field" in terms of strategies to compensate for areas of difficulty for students with disabilities. Here are some examples of in-structional or classroom accommodations that can be documented in an IEP or Section 504 Plan:

- Preferential seating or sitting near the teacher or away from distractions
- Advanced organizers: clear, visual aids with specific instructions or class outlines
- Providing adequate time for the student to respond
- Reduction in number of practice items, assignments, or tests
- Note-taking assistance or access to teacher or peer notes
- Extended or additional time on assignments and/or tests
- Providing alternative methods for student responses

It is important to note that you may not need all the examples shown above, but most students with disabilities will need a number of different supports to be successful in their classes (Adreon & Stella, 2001). Just be aware that they are there if or when you need them!

During your first year of high school, it will be important to conduct an IEP meeting where you can have the opportunity to provide input to the IEP team about how you feel you are performing in your classes. The fol-lowing are suggested questions that should be addressed by you and your IEP team:

- What do you find helpful in learning the content in your classes (e.g., working with a buddy, working one-on-one with the teacher, working in small groups)?
- What assignments are you struggling with in your classes (e.g., long essay or fill-in the blank exams, reading stories or textbooks, planning for projects or reports)?

- Have you initiated finding assistance or help for your assignments (e.g., working with the general or special education teachers, tutoring, study groups, or peer mentoring)?
- Are you or your teachers implementing your instructional accommodations outlined in your IEP?

The answers to these questions can provide very important information not only for the IEP team, but for your general and special education teachers as well. Remember that your teachers do not want to see you or any of their students being unsuccessful in their classes. They know that successful experiences lead to additional accomplishments.

RECOMMENDATIONS

High school is a time when you will make a number of lifelong memories; it is an experience like no other. Here are some tips for you and the IEP team to keep in mind when you are preparing for your first year of high school:

- The student, teachers, and parents need to develop clear and effective communication from school to home and vice versa.
- School personnel, including administrators, general and special education teachers, and other related service providers, should develop effective collaborative and communicative relationships to effectively exchange ideas and implement supportive and effective teaching practices.
- Students with disabilities should have continuous support from teachers and staff during the transition and after they have entered high school. (Letrello & Miles, 2003).
- Students should be encouraged to participate and get involved in extracurricular activities (Letrello & Miles, 2003).
- Encouragement and support from parents is essential (Kotering & Braziel, 2002).

The transition experience can seem overwhelming, but it does not have to be that way! You are reaching a new level of freedom, and with additional freedom comes additional responsibility. It is important for you to actively participate in your education. The first step is to attend and give input during your IEP meetings. The IEP team wants to hear about your thoughts, dreams, and ideas. After all, the "I" in IEP stands for "Individualized." That individual is you. You are an integral piece in the IEP process and it cannot work effectively without you!

REFERENCES

Adreon, D. & Stella, J. (2001). Transition to middle and high school: Increasing the success of students with Asperger's syndrome. *Intervention and School Clinic*, 36(5), 266–272.

Bakken, T. & Kotering, L. (1999). The constitutional and statutory obligations of schools to prevent students with disabilities from dropping out. *Remedial and Special Education, 20*(6), 360–367.

Black, S. (1999). Major school transitions require more than a one-shot orientation. *American School Board Journal, 186*, 53–55.

Deshler, D., Schumaker, J., Bulgren, J., Lenz, K., Jantzen, J.E., Adams, G., Carnine, D., Grossen, B., Davis, B. & Marquis, J. (2001). Making learning easier: Connecting new knowledge to things students already know. *Teaching Exceptional Children, 33*(4), 82–85.

Gove, P.B. (1993). *Webster's Third New International Dictionary of the English Language, Unabridged.* Springfield, MA: Merriam-Webster Inc.

Kokoszka, R. & Drye, J. (1981). Toward the least restrictive environment: High School L.D. students. *Journal of Learning Disabilities, 14*(1), 22–26.

Kotering, L. & Braziel, P. (2002). A look at youth programs as perceived by youth with learning disabilities. *Learning Disability Quarterly, 25*, 177–188.

Lanford, A.D. & Cary, L.G. (2000). Graduation requirements for students with disabilities legal and practice considerations. *Remedial and Special Education, 21*(3), 152–155.

Letrello, T.M. & Miles, D.D. (2003). The transition from middle school to high school. *Clearing House, 76*(4), 212–215.

Nuehring, M.L. & Sitlington, P.L. (2003). Moving from high school to an adult vocational provider. *Journal of Disability Policy Studies, 14*(1), 23–25.

Thurlow, M.L., Elliott, J.E. & Ysseldyke, J.E. (1998). *Testing students with disabilities: Practical strategies for complying with district and state requirements.* Thousand Oaks: Corwin.

Wiles, J. & Bondi, J. (2002). *Curriculum development.* Upper Saddle River, NJ: Merrill Prentice Hall.

Managing Educational Supports: Advice from Students with Disabilities

Ann I. Nevin with Stephen, Jamie, and Joanie

No one would argue with the idea that acceptance of uniqueness is better than rejection. However, if you are a young person with special needs, you have probably received a whole range of reactions that did not feel quite like acceptance. Perhaps you have seen someone look at you in a confused manner because your speech is difficult to understand, or maybe they stared at you with pity or compassion because you use a wheelchair or crutches. Perhaps you have worked in a group with others and realized that no one wanted to choose you to work with them. Or worse, you were accepted as a group member, but others decided that your contribution wasn't good enough and redid your work or did not even include it in the final report. But perhaps the worst possible situation is when other people make decisions about you—where you will go to school, what you will study, and where you will live—without including you in the discussion. Nevertheless, exactly that situation occurs every day in public schools. Children and teenagers with disabilities and special needs, perhaps very similar to your own, are not included at the decision table for their own Individual Education Programs (IEPs).

The U.S. Congress has passed laws (e.g., the Americans with Disabilities Act, the Individuals with Disabilities Education Act, and Section 504 of the Rehabilitation Act) that demand the inclusion of people with disabilities when deciding their educational needs. Even so, many high school students, especially those with disabilities, are *not* informed about the nature of their disabilities or the accommodations and adaptations that educators can make to improve their learning outcomes. They are not taught the self-advocacy skills that can empower them to take charge of their own educational programs.[1] Without this information, students with disabilities who transition from high school to the world of work, or the world of postsecondary education such as college or professional school, will not be able to access the hard-won rights that accrue as a result of recent legislation.

People with disabilities and their advocates have developed curriculum to teach children and youth to be more self-determined and to participate meaningfully in developing their own IEPs (Hapner & Imel, 2002; McGahey-Kovac, 2001). Students, many like you, have learned to manage their own educational supports while in high school and beyond. Listen to how Jamie, Joanie, and Stephen learned to advocate for themselves:

Jamie, a teenage girl with cerebral palsy and mild mental retardation, used the power of educational technology to help her high school teachers listen to her. Jamie's mother, Lisa, wrote this note to explain the context for Jamie's IEP meeting: "Jamie is participating more and more in her own schooling decisions. We meet periodically throughout the year with her special education support teacher. Jamie actually led her IEP last year with preparation and support."

During Jamie's sophomore year, she took a class that included Power-Point (presentation software), so she prepared for her IEP meeting as her class project. Her mother explained, "Last year when she took the technology class, the teacher considered PowerPoint too sophisticated for her (without asking me or her!). I love that she can show them what she can do!" This is what Jamie says are her strengths and goals:

I'm nice. I'm friendly to other people. Sometimes I'm funny. I'm good at singing and dancing. I like eating lunch with my friends at school. I like PE because it's fun. I was great at drumming with Mr. A. I liked learning about nutrition with Ms. R. I liked learning about weather and animals in science class this year.

Some jobs I'd like to try while I'm still in high school: Taking care of cats (cat sitting—not a veterinarian's office), babysitting, or taking care of kids in the hospital—maybe six- or seven-year-olds. Or working in the library—maybe the Escondido Public Library in the children's section. When I graduate from high school, I might like to take classes to be a doctor or a nurse.

The teachers and specialists paid attention to what Jamie had to say, especially in designing her schedule of classes, and they set up the supports that she requested:

Give me notes ahead of time before lectures or fill-in-the-blank forms so I can take notes myself; let me watch movies about the subject; let me ask someone to help me figure out the work, when I need them to; let me ask someone to write down answers for me when there is a lot of writing to do.

Jamie knew that she would need educational supports for her music class, too. Here is what she requested:

I need someone to take notes; I need help with the in-class assignments; I have to guess on all the assignments, including film notes and worksheet—it feels bad, like I don't understand it, but I still get good grades; I want to understand musical notes better, especially whole, half, quarter notes.

It has been a long-term process for Jamie to build her self-advocacy skills. She started out by just coming to the IEP meetings with her parents during fifth and sixth grade. But, actually participating in her IEP and other meetings has been a challenge. Speaking in front of groups can be a pretty disorienting experience for Jamie. During her sophomore year in high school, when she presented the PowerPoint slides at the IEP meeting, the prepared visuals actually helped her voice her own ideas because she could read what she had written. The teachers and specialists referred to the slides consistently throughout the meeting to determine Jamie's goals, adaptations, accommodations, and other educational supports. Jamie's next step is to ask for specific educational supports that will allow her to take the high school exit examinations during her senior year.

Joanie is a 2001 high school graduate with learning disabilities in reading and written expression, who also has health challenges. She first realized that she had a learning disability when she was a freshman in high school, even though she had attended special education classes throughout elementary school. She was enrolled in an English class taught by Ms. Hapner, a special educator. Ms. Hapner designed her lessons to help everyone achieve the state standards for writing essays by having each student in the class read and understand his or her Individual Education Program. They each researched the nature of their disability by going to the National Information Center for Handicapped Children and Youth Web site (http://www.nichcy.org). Then, they wrote essays describing their strengths and needs, their goals, and the educational supports they required to learn. In Joanie's words,

[When] Ms. Hapner began to explain the laws and what a disability is, I was surprised because I thought that [having a learning disability] meant I was different from everyone else. This also upset me because I thought that if people found out, that I would be left out of everything that other normal kids or teens got to do. I just didn't want to be an outcast among my peers. I think it is MOST IMPORTANT for students to learn about their special needs because it can help them to help teachers know what is going on. Just let your teachers know you have a disability and you need help with stuff from time to time. See, what helped me get over my shyness is when I got sick with a cancer called Hodgkin's lymphoma. I had to hold a meeting about what I needed to help me through my senior year in high school. I learned how to be a self-advocate. I would look up information [on the Web] on what was going on with my illness and ask my doctor questions about what was going on and what I can do to help them help me.

When asked what advice she has for other high school students, Joanie wrote,

I think it is MOST IMPORTANT to know about the laws that help students with special needs in school, especially to stand up for what you believe in and what you need. You are the only one that knows what it will take for you to succeed in your future. See, teachers help you learn what is important [but] your part is [to learn what] you can do to help progress. All you have to do is speak up for yourself and ask what you can do about your disability to improve and take control. My advice is to look up what your disability is and attend the meetings that are being held about you and voice an opinion. Also, find out what the meeting would be about and [practice] how to express yourself. Have a voice; speak up, and try not to be shy.

Joanie is very grateful for the opportunities that helped her become a self-advocate. She joined a leadership club in high school to help other teenagers learn to manage their IEPs, and she has given speeches about her experiences. She graduated from high school more than a year ago, and is now employed. She uses her self-advocacy in many ways. She explains,

After this [Hodgkin's lymphoma and subsequent chemotherapy and recovery] happened to me, I realized [life] is going to be totally different from now on. I mean, no more pity stuff in my life and no more bad relationships. I will live my life to the fullest no matter what. [I still use] the self-advocacy [skills] that I learned [while in high school]. If I have a problem with something to do with work, I ask for help and things with any problem I have. Then I ask how to do it a little better.

Stephen, a college student with autism, is an accomplished self-advocate who has given keynote addresses at state and national conferences. He explains,

I would like to say that I am 24 years old and have grown up in the disability system. I have autism. I currently attend San Diego State University and my major is computer science. I am also a technician for City Heights Educational Pilot, a nonprofit educational program funded by SDSU Foundation and Price Charities that work with some inner-city schools.

Stephen recommends that high school students with disabilities consider a whole range of options as part of their transition to post–high school life, including college, employment, internships, and other services such as drivers' education and training for using public transportation. He wrote, "Contrary to belief, many colleges, both public and private, are now accepting people with disabilities, and providing accommodations for people with disabilities in their classes. This is wonderful news: 10 years ago, not many people with disabilities went to college."

Stephen is especially articulate about the need to include specific plans for developing a social network of friends. He states,

One of the important factors of life after high school is to have a social life. This includes things like going to the movies, going to the theatre, to the ball games, to the museums, to nightclubs, to go out to eat, to go bowling, and many other fun activities. After all, what would life be without them? Sadly, I see many people with disabilities end up not having friends. This needs to be changed, and if necessary, ask to learn social and friendship skills [in the IEP]. Personally, I think this needs to start in kindergarten or preschool and continue all through life. For example, I did not know what else there was to school until I was asked to go to homecoming in grade 12. I found it sad how much I missed all those years.

When Stephen himself asked for social skills training, he had to battle the system to get it. He notes,

For example, when I requested social skills training, the school system said they had no one to teach that, yet my social skills teacher is available through the regional center. It was luck that I found her by meeting her in the tech booth for a show I did tech crew for. A lot of people I know said they have to go to due process hearings to get what they need.

Stephen clearly believes it is his right to guide his own life. He thinks the public school system should allow the person with the disability to control decisions. Stephen explains,

After all, it is my life. I should be able to get what I value the most out of it. Let me choose the path. Respect and guide and assist me on taking it. I should have a great four- to 12-year journey from high school graduation through college into the work world and into the life of an adult.

What's so special about Jamie, Joanie, and Stephen? First, they are real teenagers, just like you. Second, they had feelings that you might be having, such as confusion, worthlessness, and fear of the future. But, you might be thinking, what if your special needs are different from theirs?

What if you had muscular dystrophy, like Denise,[2] who is an adult and a coordinator of Outreach Education at a university disabilities resource center? She reported that in elementary school, due to her disability, she was home-schooled and later, although wheelchair mobile, was allowed to go to high school only part of the day due to a perception that her wheelchair would endanger her classmates. She explains,

I was a strong-willed woman [but] I was not aware of my disability and what else was out there. So, in my senior year, I decided to go looking and went to find out more accurately what my medical diagnosis was. I started looking into this movement . . . so called independent living. [My advice is] know all that you can about the realities, the necessity of accommodations and *be prepared to get the accommodation* to the extent that it is necessary.

Gena, a secondary education teacher candidate, was only a teenager when she was labeled a bipolar schizophrenic, alcoholic, and drug addict:

I think that teachers have a habit of ignoring my voice. I know that I made certain cries for help that were quite large. I mean I was not messing around. I actually attempted suicide on the school campus. I gave my suicide note to my English teacher and she read it. And you know, she was obviously made very uncomfortable, and she just said, "Why did you give this to me?"

Diane was diagnosed with learning disabilities as a teenager. Now an elementary teacher, she was attending graduate school to earn an endorsement to teach English as a second language when she explained her journey towards self-advocacy:

[I was] a junior in high school when I was diagnosed with my learning disability. I felt very worthless before that. Because of my learning disability, I was always told I could never teach. It wasn't until I was in my late thirties that somebody [a college teacher!] convinced me that I would make a good teacher. If I can't be the best, then I don't want to be here.

Only you can answer why the life experiences reported by Diane, Denise, and Gena are important, and how you personally might find them especially empowering and inspiring. Perhaps you agree that they prove it's never too late to learn about your disability, the supports you have a right to receive, and the role of your own determination in obtaining what you need. Diane became aware of a new way of thinking about her learning disability: "I can with support." Denise's drive to learn more about her disability led her to become an activist in independent living, as well as to a career in a university disability resource center helping others overcome barriers to accessing higher education. Gena used her life experience as a teenager to motivate herself to become a teacher who would have a different response to troubled teens.

Other teenagers with disabilities suggest that there are specific steps you can take immediately, such as creating a community of advocates (Moyer, 2000), reaching out to your community, taking steps to be more self-determined, and learning to lead your own IEP. Each of these actions is described in more detail below.

CREATE A COMMUNITY OF ADVOCATES

For example, review the information available at "The Arc's Self-Advocacy Activities," a well-researched up-to-date resource maintained by the Arc, an organization formerly known as the National Association for Retarded Citizens, at this address: http://www.thearc.org/misc/sadescr. html. Links to the Directory of Self-Advocacy Groups, as well as a list of videos and other self-advocacy resources from various organizations are included.

REACH OUT TO YOUR COMMUNITY

You can be inspired by many sources. There might be members in your school or church who have a disability just like yours and who might have important advice to offer. In fact, you could be an inspiration yourself by volunteering to be a tutor or a big brother/sister to a younger child who has a special need. Or you might discover, through reading a book such as *Somebody Somewhere* by Donna Williams or watching movies (e.g., *The Miracle Worker*, *Mr. Holland's Opus*, and *Dead Poet's Society*) that people with disabilities similar to your own (or very different from your own) have grown up to be successful adults. If you surf the World Wide Web, you might meet a young man like Michael Regos, who chronicles his achievements at http://www.home.vicnet.net.au/~dealccinc/Regoswel.htm. He writes, "An extra chromosome makes you better than average, not worse. I'm trying to live like a human being, not a person with Down syndrome."

Many high school students with disabilities and their parents and advocates have worked with the Institute for Community Inclusion (Timmons, Moloney, Dreilinger & Schuster, 2002). They discovered that personal networks are a good way to increase the feeling of being independent and capable in real life. They suggest that you:

Ask for help when you face big decisions in your life. Talk or write to tell people what you are thinking, share your goals, and your fears. Be specific about how you want people to help you. Feel free to ask different people if at first you do not receive the help you need to make your dreams a reality.

TAKE STEPS TO BECOME SELF-DETERMINED

There are many ways to gain the skills you need to become a self-advocate—to learn about yourself and to value your strengths so that you can set reasonable goals and take appropriate action to reach them. Join a group or start one of your own! Ask a trusted counselor, teacher, or family member to review with you the several fine commercially available programs. For example, Sharon Field and Alan Hoffman at Wayne State University worked with teachers and students like you to field test the "Steps to Self-Determination" curriculum (Field & Hoffman, 2002). If you want to increase your ability to identify and achieve goals based on a foundation of knowing and valuing yourself, then this might be the program that fits you. (Visit the *Self-Determination and Transition Projects*

Web site at http://www.coe.wayne.edu/Grants/STEPS/index.htm for more information.)

In addition to specific curriculum, there are also teaching strategies that might help you. Become more aware of the types of accommodations that might assist your learning. For example, you can ask your special education teacher, advocate, or family member to review different ways of teaching the classes you take in school. There are many teaching strategies that your high school and college teachers might find interesting. For example, a middle school English teacher implemented literature circles to help eighth and ninth graders analyze literature selections (Blum, Lipsitt, & Yokum, 2002). The teenagers used their choice-making skills (an important component of self-determination) to select what they read and the themes they discussed. Because the students and the teacher would grade participation, the students learned specific roles to practice during the literature circle meetings. They could be an illustrator, task organizer, scribe, or a connector (a person who found connections between the book and the world outside). Some of the students in the class had special needs similar to yours, such as learning disabilities in written expression, hearing impairments, reading disabilities, and Attention Deficit Hyperactivity Disorder. But the literature circles helped the students with special needs in the class to show significant changes in their ability to understand, remember, and explain what they had read.

LEARN TO LEAD YOUR IEP MEETINGS

Ask your special educator to help you learn to manage your own IEP process. Like Joanie, you can start by learning more about your own disability and about the laws that protect you. Your teachers can use the lessons developed by Marcy McGahey-Kovac (2001) in *A Student's Guide to the IEP* (available free from the NICHCY Web site), or the lessons developed by Hapner and Imel (2002). Hapner and Imel (2002) explained that some of the benefits you can expect from this process include better decision-making skills, similar to what Juan, a 17-year-old with learning disabilities found: "[The teachers] gave me the chance to make decisions on my own" (p. 123). Raul, an 18-year-old with expressive and receptive language processing disabilities, asked to stay after school to study the driver's manual with his special educator so he could pass the test to receive his license. Raul said, "Teachers started to listen and show respect" (p. 126).

You might discover new rights, similar to Peter, a 16-year-old with learning disabilities, "I learned the laws—I learned that we can do some things others can't, like we can stay in high school 'til we are 22" (p. 126). Self-knowledge and valuing oneself can also change, like Juan who wrote, "In my student-led IEP, I felt more comfortable knowing that I can accept the fact that I have a disability. I graduated eighth grade feeling proud of myself for working hard on how I can improve [even with] my disability" (p. 126).

CONCLUSION

We fervently hope you are inspired by our stories and that you are motivated to go far beyond what you may perceive are your limitations at this point in time. We know, and hope you are also now aware, that you *can* learn to talk so that your teachers will listen. You *can* learn what to say to achieve what you want or need to have your dreams become a reality. You *can* learn to ask the right questions and to keep asking until you hear the answers you want!

Perhaps you'll agree with Burton Blatt, a pioneer in the liberation of people with disabilities, who wrote, "Optimism is not in believing that things will turn out well, objectively. But in believing that one can face things, subjectively, however they turn out. Optimism is not in feeling good, but in feeling that good has a chance to survive."[3]

NOTES

1. Professor Michael Wehmeyer, codeveloper of a self-determination assessment profile, has found that "Out of nearly 900 transition related goals, there were none that indicated students were being taught the skills they need to make choices, solve problems, make decisions, set and achieve goals, or understand themselves" (Wehmeyer & Schwartz, 1998, p. 82).

2. Excerpts from Denise, Gena, and Diane are more fully reported in Nevin et al., 2002.

3. As cited in Taylor, S. & Blatt, S. (1999). *In search of the Promised Land: The collected papers of Burton Blatt*. Washington, DC: American Association for Mental Retardation.

REFERENCES

Adults with Disabilities Act resource guide. (2002). Available online: http://www.nwbuildnet.com/nwbn/ada.html (retrieved February 7, 2003).

Blum, H.T., Lipsitt, L. & Yokom, D. (2002). Literature circles: A tool for self-determination in one middle school inclusive classroom. *Remedial and Special Education, 23*(2), 99–108.

Field, S. & Hoffman, A. (2002). Lessons learned from implementing the Steps to Self-Determination curriculum. *Remedial and Special Education, 23*(2), 90–99.

Hapner, A. & Imel, B. (2002). Voices of students with disabilities: "Teachers started to listen and show respect." *Remedial and Special Education, 23*(2), 122–126.

Hinckle, S. (2002, July). Advice for life AFTER high school. Presentation at 3rd Annual Leadership Conference, California State University, San Marcos, CA.

Houghtelin, Jamie. (2002, July). Using technology to help me explain my strengths, needs, goals, and accommodations. Presentation at 3rd Annual Leadership Conference, California State University, San Marcos, CA (with J. Thousand and L. Houghtelin).

Individuals with Disabilities Education Act of 1997 resource guide. (2002). Available online: http://www.dssc.org/frc/idea.htm (maintained by the Federal Resource Center for Special Education; retrieved February 7, 2003).

Kluth, P. (1999, December). Developing successful schooling experiences for facilitative communication (FC) users: An interview with Franklin and Pat Wilson. *Facilitative Communication Institute Newsletter, 8*(1), 7–11. Available online: http://www.soeweb.syr.edu/thefci/7-2klu.htm.

McGahey-Kovac, M. (2001). *A student's guide to the IEP*. Reston, VA: Council for Exceptional Children. Available (free) at National Information Center for Handicapped Children and Youth (NICHCY) Web site: http://www.nichcy.org/pubs/stuguide/st1.htm.

Moyer, J. (2000). *How big is your circle? A musical promoting healing of exclusion, ridicule and violence*. Compact Disk, script, and activity guide. Cleveland, OH: Jeff Moyer Music.

National Information Center for Handicapped Children and Youth. Maintains up-to-date fact sheets for a wide range of disability categories. Available online: http://www.nichcy.org.

Nevin, A., Cardelle-Elawar, M., Beckett, C., Thousand, J. & Diaz-Greenberg, R. (2002). Eliciting and taking action on the voices of adults with disabilities: Advice for teacher education professors. *Journal of Professional Studies, 9*(2), 70–79.

Regos, M. *Up Down syndrome!* Available online: http://www.home.vicnet. net.au/ ~dealccinc/Regoswel.htm.

Section 504 of the 1973 Rehabilitation Act explained. (2002). Available online: http://www.spot.pcc.edu/osd/504.htm (maintained by the U.S. Office for Students with Disabilities; retrieved February 7, 2003).

Timmons, J., Moloney, M., Dreilinger, D. & Schuster, J. (2002, September/October). Making dreams a reality: Using personal networks to achieve goals as you prepare to leave high school. *TASH Connections, 28*(9/10), 1–6.

Wehmeyer, M. & Schwartz, M. (1998). The self-determination focus of transition goals for students with mental retardation. *Career Development of Exceptional Individuals*, 75–85.

Williams, D. (1995). *Somebody somewhere: Breaking free from the world of autism*. New York: Times Books.

Curriculum: To Run the Race

Cynthia Ann Bowman

INTRODUCTION

The term curriculum has its origins in the running and chariot tracks of ancient Greece. Thousands of years ago, curriculum was, literally, a course to
run. In ancient Rome, curriculum was a racing chariot; *currere* was to run in
Latin. Greek philosopher Aristotle categorized knowledge into three separate disciplines: the theoretical, the productive, and the practical. As such,
when people discuss "curriculum," they are not talking about a physical
object; instead, they are referring to the interactions between educators,
students, and the knowledge they are studying. Curriculum goes beyond
situating the learning experience simply within the experience of the
learner. It is a process that incorporates the experiences of both the learner
and the teacher and, through dialogue and negotiation, draws upon both.
This process encourages students and teachers to work together to confront the real problems of their existence and relationships.

WHAT IS TYPICAL IN HIGH SCHOOL CURRICULUM?

Although specific graduation requirements vary from one state to another, the typical course of study is about 22 credits earned in grades 9–12
to meet minimum requirements and qualify for graduation. A typical se-
quence might look like this:

Grade 9

English—1 full year
Social Studies—1 full year

Science—1 full year
Algebra/Transition Math—1 full year
Physical Education—1 full year
Keyboarding I—1/2 semester

Grade 10

English—1 full year
American History—1 full year
Physical Education/Health—1 full year

Grades 10–12

Science Electives—1 (2 semesters)
Math Electives—1 (2 semesters)
Other Electives (grades 9–12)—7 (14 semesters)

Grade 11

Communications—1/2 semester
American Literature/Technical Writing—1/2 semester
World History—1/2 semester
World Geography/Affairs—1/2 semester

Grade 12

English: One of several options—1 full year
Social Studies: American Government—1/2 semester
and American Political System—1/2 semester
Health—1/2 semester

THE CLASSROOM ENVIRONMENT

The task for the student with disabilities in the regular classroom environment is difficult, especially for those with auditory, attention, auditory processing, or comprehension problems. Students must have access to multiple sources of information that are audible and/or visible to improve understanding and comprehension. Under conditions of a regular classroom, the student and teacher must engage in a process of communication, most of it emanating from the teacher. Assuming that opportunity and motivation are high, the process can, nonetheless, be undermined by poor instruction.

Even if the instructional quality is also high, any environmental problem—notably noise and lack of visual cues—can still cause the process to collapse. Instructional strategies—deductive and inductive methods, lectures, questions, and practice, as well as group and discussion methods—are critically dependent upon the ability to hear and see clearly and to comprehend.

Modification of Instruction

Few high schools have adopted student-centered models because the most common innovation in recent years has been the tendency to experiment with "time" models, such as various block-scheduling techniques. It is also less likely that there will be "team" teaching between classroom and special education teachers. The resource room model and/or the consulting model of special education delivery are likely to be the preferred options, although continuing litigation, court decisions, and financial complications may cause more school districts to consider inclusion in secondary schools. Yeager (1995) reported that teachers who are educated in using various teaching strategies, such as advanced organizers, study guides, visual organizers, and learning strategies, provide better instruction for all students in an inclusive classroom.

Topical Outlines

A topical outline is a simple device that can provide significant information to students and parents. Clarifying what content will be covered in a unit or section is easily done by these methods:

- *Glossaries and Summaries*—A glossary can be useful in any kind of subject matter or content. Students are going to encounter many unfamiliar terms, and this is one way of modifying direct instruction that does not require a great deal of the teacher's time.
- *Cognitive Organizers*—Like prereading questions, cognitive organizers can be used with a unit of instruction to prepare students for the "big ideas" to be examined in the course of study.
- *Study Guides*—A true study guide is a comprehensive manual of all assignments, expectations, and information about "due dates" and examinations. Study guides can be helpful to parents and tutors who work with students.
- *Visual Aids*—Too much reliance on oral presentation in the classroom can defeat the instructional goals of the teacher, but the use of visual illustrations can enhance the presentation. Any kind of visual information offered by the teacher to accompany the lesson can support the major points presented, maintain attention, and improve comprehension. Graphics, actual scenes, pictures, and large text fonts can produce higher achievement and assist students in generating mental frameworks of knowledge.

- *Acoustical Treatment*—A good acoustical treatment or amplification of the teacher's voice in the classroom can do much to improve clarity and understanding. This is especially effective in secondary classrooms, which are larger and may have more students.

- *Homework*—Completing homework and bringing the appropriate materials to class may be indications of the student's motivation. If the majority of students are prepared, teachers can devote most of their time to teaching. Most subjects in secondary school have a great deal of assigned homework. Depending upon the needs and abilities of the student as expressed in the Individualized Education Program (IEP), homework should be reasonable and its purposes clearly related to instructional goals.

Testing and Alternative Assessment

Many secondary school classes base evaluation on teacher-made tests, usually in objective formats. Alternatives to these tests, which may benefit all students, include three types of performance-based assessment: performances, portfolios, and projects.

- *Performances*—According to Price and Marsh (1995), performance may be simple or complex, intermediate or summative. A child may demonstrate knowledge of addition (regrouping) by using concrete objects instead of a test item on a paper. A student may classify objects, such as Venn diagrams, plants, or animals, or perform more complex tasks, such as setting up a database. Rather than taking a printed test to check reading skills, for example, the child may read (perform) a passage or tape-record oral reading. Recitations, oral reports, and group presentations lend themselves to performances in social studies, foreign languages, mathematics, science, and other parts of the curriculum. This can vary with the imagination of the teacher and the students. Any knowledge or skill that can be demonstrated may have the potential for a performance: oral presentation, lab demonstration, reading, debate, dance, or dramatization.

- *Portfolios*—Portfolio assessment is appropriate for ongoing evaluation, such as writing, reading, and fine arts skills. The portfolio, which may be nothing more than a box, physically stores a student's work over a long period of time, and can include written material as well as video or audiotapes of performances. Portfolios are used for science, mathematics, language arts, literacy, and the arts, and might include samples of a student's paintings, drawings, sculpture, photographs, stories, letters, poems, lists, signs, handwriting, and use of numbers. Gathered frequently over a period of time, portfolios can serve as a collection of work to show a student's achievements. Because they are based on multiple sources of information from a year or several years in the school setting, the work can give a developmental history of the pupil and lead to predictions about potential. The documentation amassed in a collection can contain both the student's everyday work, as well as his or her greatest accomplishments. An active portfolio assessment will soon take up much space, requiring considerations to be made about how long items are kept. As technology is becoming more available and affordable, it is possible to store many items in a secondary format, such as videotape or digitized video. Sophisticated development of assessment items may also improve delivery and use of items for teachers (Price & Marsh, 1995).

- *Projects*—Projects may be used to assess a student's ability to reason, gather and organize facts and ideas, and to provide an integrated work. A project may utilize an approach that entails the presentation of a problem that must be solved by applying theories and formulas. Such problem-solving approaches, for example, can be applied in science, math, and social studies. A project can consist of a short-term or long-term activity for an individual student or a team that results in a product that represents some considerable effort. Depending upon the teacher's goals and the student's capabilities or interests, projects can be very simple or quite complex. Either as a separate subject area or an integrated product, a project can be prepared in many forms. Students can create original written works, photographic essays, musical productions, dances, and technical-type papers (Price & Marsh, 1995).

Considerations for Classroom Instruction

Regardless of the program or nature of the class, at the secondary level, students will be required or expected to read, listen, and take notes in class.

Attending to Lectures/Discussions

Long lectures highlight a main problem for the adjustment of many students with disabilities at the secondary level. In the elementary grades, there are workstations, work centers, small groups, and a variety of activities. Contrastingly, in many secondary classrooms, there is just one large class usually listening to and watching the teacher. In this situation, most problems can be expected for many students with disabilities, especially those who cannot understand what the teacher is talking about or who cannot pay attention for an entire class period or enter into classroom discussions. Although the courts have ruled that teachers must adjust their instruction to accommodate such differences, many still regard this as totally inappropriate. Not knowing how to organize instruction any other way, many teachers do not consider the fact that the classroom could be set up differently, such as using learning centers instead of lectures.

Note Taking

Students are usually expected to maintain notes on classroom activities, although there may be little effort to teach them how and why notes are taken. Many students will not be able to take notes because of a variety of impairments. Alternatives may be used, such as having someone share notes with the student or by making tape recordings. Both of these techniques are less than satisfactory due to the unreliability of note takers and the fact that some teachers dislike being recorded. Also, tape recordings are not helpful because the student has to literally listen to the entire class all over again, like sitting through class twice.

Grading

For students with disabilities, as a result of the IEP, it should be possible to insist that the student's performance be listed in terms of progress toward specific objectives. This could be a list of skills or checklist, portfolios, participation in class discussion, class projects, oral reports, anecdotal records of student performance, daily logs of student activities, and modified tests. Teachers and parents will be concerned about how students will be evaluated in the classroom, especially with respect to grading practices, and if the IEP will include a component to evaluate the teacher's compliance with the program. Grading may also raise certain questions in discussions between the members of the IEP team. Should students with disabilities, who are given consultation and mentoring through some type of enrichment and/or academic support program, be allowed to receive the same grades as students who receive no special assistance? Should students with disabilities be required to compete with nondisabled peers? Does the IEP, which determines the expected outcomes, dictate a grade if objectives are met?

The school should assure that the grading and testing procedures employed do not reflect the child's disability and that the student has ample opportunity to learn the skills and demonstrate competence, even if through alternative means.

MODIFICATION BY MEANS OF STUDENT-CENTERED LEARNING MODELS

Individualized Learning Situations

A student who is provided with a comprehensive learning guide may progress through a curriculum at his or her own rate. Not bound by the class schedule, an advanced student can move quickly and progress toward more complex subject matter. For those with slower paces, the flexibility of deadlines for marking progress and completing assignments reduces stress and anxiety. While this may be more useful in schools that have some form of block scheduling, it can still be used in a traditional high school setting. Built into the guide would be all assignments, activities, explanations, and even ways to complete specific tasks, such as meeting with peer groups, small groups, and completing individual activities.

Year-Round Schooling

Year-round education is an alternative to the traditional nine-month school year, partly for economic reasons. While school enrollments at the elementary level are increasing, communities are much less willing to support tax increases to build new facilities. By adopting a year-round model, schools can offer education more economically and without expansion. This may provide more options for families of children with disabilities, who may plan activities over 12 months instead of only nine.

The School Within a School

It is especially popular to organize large schools as if there are several independent educational communities that happen to share the same facility. Each "school" has the flexibility to have its own curriculum, personnel, and way of organizing. The students may spend a number of years with the same peers and the same teachers, developing a sense of community. Other options can be used within this context, depending on each "school," including individualization, continuous progress, and adjusting for needs of pupils with disabilities (McLeod, 1996). This model can be useful at the secondary level for accommodating the needs of many students with disabilities.

ADVICE TO HIGH SCHOOL STUDENTS WITH DISABILITIES

Following are some important things for high school students with disabilities to remember:

- Understand your disability, including its effect on learning and work.
- Establish ambitious, meaningful, and realistic goals.
- Present a positive self-image by stressing strengths.
- Understand the influence of the disability.
- Develop and apply effective strategies for studying, test taking, time management, and note taking.
- Know your rights and responsibilities that are necessary to prepare for and to access postsecondary education (NJCLD, 1994).

WHILE YOU ARE STILL IN HIGH SCHOOL

While still in school, there are things you can do to prepare for a career and make the transition from school to work easier. At the latest, transition planning should begin at age 14 for students with disabilities. If you are 16 or older, there must be a statement of needed transition services included in your IEP. Transition, broadly defined, is an all-inclusive process that focuses on improving a student's employment outcomes, housing options, and social networks after leaving school. The transition plan provides the framework for identifying, planning, and carrying out activities that will help you make a successful move to adult life. Some options after high school, according to the Learning Disabilities Association of America (http://www.ldanatl.org), might include postsecondary education, vocational training, integrated employment, continuing and adult education services, independent living, or community experiences. The plan identifies the types of skills to be learned, as well as which transition services will be provided, when they will be provided, and the party responsible for providing them. Involving a team of people drawn from different parts of your school and community life, the transition process focuses on your unique needs and goals (NTN, 1996).

Your specific needs for postsecondary (after high school) services should determine who is invited to the IEP transition meeting. It is important to include representatives from the appropriate adult agencies and organizations, such as mental health, vocational rehabilitation, housing, employment and training, and community colleges. By law, you also have to be invited to your IEP meeting and involved in your transition planning. To begin the process, think about your interests, skills, and desires for the future. Here are some activities you may wish to consider while preparing transition plans with the IEP team. Ask yourself whether or not these issues should be discussed during the meeting (NTN, 1996):

- You should identify interests and options for future living arrangements.
- Learn to communicate effectively your interests, preferences, and needs.
- Be able to explain your disability and the accommodations you need.
- Investigate money management and identify necessary financial skills.
- Identify and begin learning skills necessary for independent living.
- Identify community support services and programs.
- Invite adult service providers, peers, and others to the IEP transition meeting.
- Match career interests and skills with course work and community work experiences.
- Gather more information on postsecondary programs and the support services offered.
- Make arrangements to take college entrance exams.
- Determine the need for financial support.
- Learn and practice appropriate interpersonal, communication, and social skills for different settings.
- Prepare a resume and update it as needed.
- Practice independent living skills (budgeting, shopping, cooking, and housekeeping).
- Apply for financial support programs.

- Identify the postsecondary school you plan to attend and arrange for accommodations.
- Specify desired job and obtain paid employment with support as needed.
- Take responsibility for arriving on time to work, appointments, and social activities.

These may seem trivial and inconsequential now amidst the challenges of high school, but, from personal experience, I can guarantee how important planning will be. Having suffered from juvenile rheumatoid arthritis since the age of five, my strengths were academic rather than athletic. I knew that to be successful I would have to go to college, but I had difficulty tying my shoes, shampooing my hair, and walking long distances. Each time I asked my parents or brother for help, they would ask how I would manage on my own in college. It seemed so far away. . . . However, I had to talk with my freshman roommate very honestly about her willingness to help me when necessary. We had never met, and it was embarrassing to explain that occasionally I would need to ask for assistance. Being told by advisers that I couldn't major in education because my disability would make classroom management impossible was unexpected and hurtful. These minor obstacles could have been avoided by careful planning and communication.

REFERENCES

McLeod, B. (1996). *School reform and student diversity: Exemplary schooling for language minority students.* The National Center for Research on Cultural Diversity and Second Language Learning. Washington, DC: U.S. Department of Education, The Office of Educational Research and Improvement (OERI).

National Information Center for Children and Youth with Disabilities (NICHCY). (1997). Options after high school for youth with disabilities. Available online: http://www.nichcy.org/pubs/transum/ts7txt.htm.

National Joint Committee on Learning Disabilities (NJCLD). (1994, January). Secondary to postsecondary education transition planning for students with learning disabilities. Available online: http://www.ldonline.org/ld_indepth/transition/njcld_transition.html.

National Transition Network (NTN). (1996). Transition planning for success in adult life. Available online: http://www.ici.coled.umn.edu/ntn/pub/briefs/tplanning.html.

Price, B.J. & Marsh, G.E. II. (1995). *Performance-based assessment in quality elementary and middle schools.* Alexandria, VA: National Association of Elementary School Principals.

Yeager, N. (1995). Inclusion: The results of attendance, achievement, and self-concept in a class model. In *Reaching to the future: Boldly facing challenges in rural communities.* Conference Proceedings of the American Council on Rural Special Education (ACRES), Las Vegas, NV, March 15–18, 1995, ERIC Document Service No. ED381334.

Libraries, Media Centers, Online Resources, and the Research Process

Tom McNulty

INTRODUCTION

Many students wonder why they are required to do some of their school assignments in the library instead of at home or at one of the computers in their classrooms. With so many things (encyclopedias, dictionaries, books, and magazines) available on the Internet, why do we have libraries at all? The truth is, there are lots of very important sources of information that you won't find on the Web—at least, not yet. That's why your school has a library, and more importantly, a librarian to help you with your work.

This chapter discusses libraries, librarians, and some of the best Internet sites that you can use for research papers and projects. Also explored are some of the challenges that the library and the Internet can present to students with disabilities. Some people have disabilities (like blindness, learning problems, low vision) that make it difficult to use books, magazines, and other printed material. For this group, some alternatives to print are considered, including Braille and large print, "talking books," digital books, and other electronic substitutes.

Using a computer can be challenging for people with many types of disabilities, but now there are a number of products that can make the computer "disability friendly." Some of these products are discussed briefly, like large-print software, speech output, voice input, and others, that make it possible for just about everyone to gain access to the world of electronic information.

Taking some time to learn how to use the library will definitely pay off—now and in the future. You'll prepare better assignments and projects, get higher grades, and have many more choices down the road if you take a little time to get to know your library and your librarian. And, hopefully, you'll even have some fun along the way!

WHY USE THE LIBRARY?

So, why is it important to get to know the library, and what exactly can the library provide that you can't find somewhere else? First, let's consider briefly why we have libraries in the first place.

Most of us own some books, subscribe to a magazine or two, and collect our favorite music and movies; we have libraries, of a sort. But very few of us have the physical space to house everything that we would like to own, or the money to buy the vast numbers of books, magazines, CDs, videos, or other media that we want to have access to. Even considering the huge number of very valuable, free-of-charge Internet sites, we still need to have access to a library in order to maximize our available resources. That's what libraries do.

And libraries aren't just random collections of things. First and probably foremost, they are collections of things that were acquired because they meet certain criteria. That is, they are of high quality, the material they present is believed to be true or valid, and they support the work of the group they are meant to serve. For example, the public library should meet the needs of the people of the town or city, and the school library, likewise, should have materials that serve the needs of students and teachers.

In addition to being of high quality, library materials are organized in such a way that they can be found, and used, conveniently. How many of us have fumbled through shelf after shelf of CDs at home, in search of a particular piece of music? With really huge collections, order is even more critical. A room full of shelves with 10,000 books would be of little use if those books were not in some meaningful order.

For your immediate needs, learning how to find and evaluate information will help you to prepare better projects and papers. That's pretty obvious. But chances are, you've heard that we're living in the "information age." That means, among other things, that the ability to find and evaluate information will be a critical skill that you'll need for the rest of your life. If you choose to go on to college, you'll be happy that you took the time to develop your research skills. But no matter what you do, you will need to be able to find and evaluate information. So, from writing an A+ term paper to selecting the right car (or just about anything else you can imagine), the ability to use a library effectively will be crucial to your success both in and out of school.

FINDING BOOKS

When most of us think of libraries, we probably still picture rows and rows of books, magazines, and other printed materials. Sure, we expect libraries to have computers too, but the good old-fashioned book has certainly not gone away. Learning how to find them, and how to use them, is a big part of learning to use the library. But before we go into the nuts and bolts of finding what we need, let's look at the types of books you can expect to find in your library.

Most libraries have books that you can check out, and some are restricted to library use, usually called "reference books." There are a few reasons why some books are designated reference; as the term implies, we refer to them, rather than curl up and read them cover-to-cover, like we would a novel or a biography. Things like directories, encyclopedias, and dictionaries are often kept as "reference only" titles, and must be used in the library. Of course, lots of these are now available electronically—a great convenience. A list of some of the better reference sources you can find on the Internet is included at the end of this chapter. Reference books, books that you can check out, magazines, and other forms of print have one thing in common: in order to be really usable, they must be easily located, and in order for that to be possible, they have to be organized.

If you think about it, there are many ways that libraries could be organized. For example, books could be arranged by their authors' names, they might be put together by size, or simply put on shelves in no particular order. Believe it or not, all of these ways of "organizing" collections have been used at some point in the long history of libraries. But today, for the most part, libraries group books and other materials together based upon their subject. Logically, this makes a collection most usable; for instance, the student who is researching history will obviously want to find history books grouped together or near one another. A collection arranged in this way makes browsing easy and effective. But in order to keep books in this order, they have to be classified. Learning how your library is classified will go a long way in helping you to find what you need.

There are a few major systems for organizing libraries, but the most widely used, especially in public and school libraries, is the Dewey Decimal Classification (DDC). This system was developed by Melvil Dewey in 1873, and is still used by countless libraries around the world. You'll probably learn the basics of the Dewey system at some point in one of your classes, maybe in connection with one of your first research paper assignments. But if DDC is new to you, here are the basics in a nutshell:

DDC: THE TEN MAIN CLASSES

Almost any book you can think of has a major subject—art, history, religion, and so forth. The Dewey Decimal Classification is a numerical system for grouping these subjects together. The Dewey number assigned to a title starts first with one of 10 very broad classes, ranging from 000 through 900:

000   Computers, information, & general reference
100   Philosophy & psychology
200   Religion
300   Social sciences
400   Language
500   Science
600   Technology
700   Arts & recreation
800   Literature
900   History & geography

So, if you're putting all of your science books together, you know that they are in the "500" range. But if we didn't divide them up further, you'd have botany books sitting next to physics books, and some chemistry, astronomy, and other science titles thrown in between. That wouldn't make it easy to browse. That's why it is important to create meaningful divisions within these big groups; the Dewey Decimal Classification does this.

The second number in our three-digit class indicates the main division (e.g., astronomy) within the larger subject (science). If we're classifying an astronomy book, we know it would start with 520—the "5" meaning science, and the "2" meaning astronomy. But what about that "0"? What if we had a very huge collection of books about astronomy, for example? Would it be enough to have these books together, or is there yet another way we'd want them grouped? That's where the third digit comes in. So, astronomy books that focus on the planet Earth are given the number 525, while books about celestial navigation go together under 527.

These numbers, commonly called "call numbers" or "class numbers," appear on the spine of each book, and are basically the book's address. They tell us where we can find any particular title among the many that make up the library. When you look up a book in your library's catalog, this is the number you'll need to easily track it down.

With a little experience, you'll find that it becomes easy, and fun, to find what you need in the library. If you're lost at the beginning, ask your librarian or teacher to help you.

USING MAGAZINES AND PERIODICALS

Some, more current, topics are covered best by articles in magazines or newspapers. For example, if you're looking for information on something that happened yesterday, or for a review of a movie that's just been released, you won't find the information you want in a book, because books take time to write and to be published. Most likely, for these kinds of topics, the information you want will be in today's newspaper or in a recently published magazine. Learning how to track down articles is another library skill that will be crucial for your success in high school and will be even more important in college.

In the days before we had computers, people found articles by using printed indexes. We still have these, but more and more, indexes appear in computerized form, and people expect to get the complete article without getting up from their computer workstation. The truth is, many magazines and newspapers are on the Web, but not all of them. Your school or local public library probably provides one or more very useful periodical databases. In larger institutions, there might be a lot to choose from. Ask your librarian which one to use for any given research topic.

SPECIAL MATERIALS FOR PEOPLE WITH DISABILITIES—AND WHERE TO FIND THEM

Although many libraries provide more than just books and magazines, these traditional formats continue to be necessary for school assignments, papers, and projects. But some students' disabilities make it difficult or impossible to use regular books, magazines, and other printed materials. People who have learning disabilities or visual impairments often use tape-recorded books ("talking books"), Braille, and other alternatives to print; but unless you happen to be in a special school for people with disabilities, don't expect to find many (or any) of these on the shelves of your school or local public library.

Students who meet certain eligibility requirements have access to a few large library systems that do provide reading materials in a variety of alternative formats. But before going into a discussion of these special libraries, let's take a look at some of the various alternatives to print that are available to students.

ALTERNATIVE FORMAT BOOKS AND MAGAZINES

Braille

For people who have very little, or no vision at all, Braille is one of the oldest alternatives to print. It was invented by Louis Braille, who became blind as a young child and attended one of the very first special schools for children with visual impairments.

People who read Braille do so by touching patterns of raised dots that represent letters and word combinations. A distinctive, six-dot "cell" represents each letter of the alphabet. The following three cells represent "a," "b," and "c." The darkened dots are raised, while the others are not:

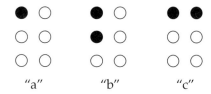

In what is referred to as Grade 2 Braille, some frequently used parts of words (called "morphemes") are given their own Braille sequences, basically to save space. For example, there are many words that end with "ment," such as "apartment," "entertainment," and "confinement," to name just a few. Therefore, in Grade 2 Braille, "ment" has just two, rather than four "cells":

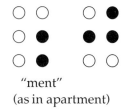

"ment"
(as in apartment)

You can see how these contractions would not only save space, but also make reading faster.

Despite its long history, there are some drawbacks to Braille. First of all, most books and magazines are not available in Braille. This is because it is expensive to produce and can be extremely bulky. The pages are thicker than regular paper, because they have raised dots on them. But even with these few drawbacks, many people continue to use Braille books and magazines.

Large Print

Most people who use Braille have very little vision or none at all. There are even larger numbers of people with some vision, but not enough to read standard print. For them, larger print is all that is required. So, how big should the print be to qualify as "large print"?

Printed letters, numbers, and characters are measured in "points." Most books, newspapers, and magazines use print that is anywhere from

8 to 12 points. Here's what some different print sizes, measured in points, look like:

This is 8-point type

This is 10-point type

This is 12-point type

This is 14-point type

This is 16-point type

This is 18-point type

Large-print books and magazines generally use 14-, 16-, or 18-point type. Large print, while very useful for many people, shares some of the drawbacks we saw with Braille. Books tend to be bulkier (though not as bulky as Braille), and most books, magazines, and newspapers are not produced in this way. However, there are lots of ways (discussed later in this chapter) that people with limited vision can make their own large print—on the computer screen itself and in paper printouts.

Talking Books

People who have visual impairments or learning disabilities often find that listening is one of the best alternatives to reading visually, and there are several organizations that produce books on tape for just this purpose. The tape-recorded book, or "talking book," dates back to the middle of the last century, when volunteers began recording books for the many soldiers and others who were blinded during World War II. This group of volunteers eventually formed an organization called "Recording for the Blind," which changed its name in the mid-1990s to "Recording for the Blind and Dyslexic" (RFB&D). RFB&D is further discussed in the next section, where we look at the organizations that make talking books and other formats available.

Electronic Texts

One of the most exciting new substitutes for printed books and magazines, the "digital book," allows people with disabilities to work in ways that would not be possible with older, less-sophisticated formats. Imagine that you were working with a very long tape-recorded book, for example, and needed to find a particular bit of information. The best you might hope for is that each chapter would begin with a certain tone, so that you could fast-forward or rewind to the beginning of the section you think you need. But to pinpoint something you need would be extremely challenging.

The digital talking book is still in its infancy, but holds great promise as the medium of the future for people with disabilities. A following section about computer technology explains how, with the right hardware and software, you'll be able to use many different types of books, magazines, newspapers, Web sites, and just about anything else you can imagine!

THE LIBRARIES

Recording for the Blind and Dyslexic (http://www.rfbd.org)

Recording for the Blind and Dyslexic (RFB&D) is one of the most important sources of nonprint educational reading material, especially for students who cannot read because of a visual, physical, or learning disability. If you fall into this category, speak with your parents, teacher, librarian, or counselor about getting a membership to RFB&D. It is not expensive, and it might be just the thing you need to really succeed in high school and beyond.

Recording for the Blind and Dyslexic's library doesn't have certain kinds of books, like the latest best-selling novels; rather, its mission is to provide materials that are educational. For recreational reading, there is another big library—the National Library Service of the Library of Congress (described below)—that produces accessible-format books and magazines for leisure reading.

In order to become a member of RFB&D, students must complete a form and present documentation of their disability. Membership comes with a number of services, including:

- Access to RFB&D's library, which has more than 93,000 titles covering a broad range of subjects, like history, literature, and the sciences. You can check to see if RFB&D has a title you're looking for by searching their catalog of titles on the Web at: http://www.rfbd.org/catalog.htm.
- Custom taping—Can't find what you need in RFB&D's catalog? Members who need a specific item can ask that it be taped for them.
- Reference help—Reference librarians are the ones who can help you to answer questions. Your membership in RFB&D allows you unlimited access to reference service.

National Library Service for the Blind and Physically Handicapped (http://www.loc.gov/nls/)

The National Library Service for the Blind and Physically Handicapped (NLS) is the branch of our national library, the Library of Congress, which produces and distributes books and magazines in special formats for people with disabilities.

NLS is very different from RFB&D in terms of what it makes available. Don't expect to find your social studies textbook here—that would be an RFB&D title. Rather, NLS is the place where you would find the Braille or recorded edition of *Harry Potter and the Sorcerer's Stone* and other best-selling novels.

Anyone with a documented disability can apply for membership and services from NLS. For information on criteria, go to the NLS Web site (http://www.loc.gov/nls/). Once you register, you'll be able to order books and magazines in Braille or on tape. Most people receive and return their books by mail, and you don't even have to pay postage!

Like RFB&D, the "talking books" produced by the Library of Congress cannot be used on a regular cassette tape player. Rather, you have to use a special playback machine that you can borrow from NLS, free of charge. You should talk with your parents, teacher, or librarian about becoming a member of NLS; if you benefit from special format books and magazines, you'll be amazed at how much you can get from the National Library Service!

To find out if NLS has a title you're interested in reading, go to their on-line catalog: http://www.loc.gov/nls/web-blnd/search.html. Note that the catalog includes lots of books that are not produced by NLS, including many from foreign countries. To limit your search to NLS items, make sure you click on the "Search for" box and select "NLS only."

TECHNOLOGY FOR PEOPLE WITH DISABILITIES

We started this chapter by talking about what libraries are, and why they continue to be important for our work. We noted that there are many things that are not available electronically, but with each day, more and more high-quality sources of information become available in computerized format.

This section examines some of the hardware and software that can make electronic information easier to use. The computer poses two basic types of obstacles to people with disabilities. If you have a visual or learning disability, for example, there are numerous programs that will make your computer talk, or that will enlarge the type to a size that is easy for you to read. If your disability makes it difficult for you to type, there are programs that allow you to write or issue commands to your computer by speaking.

Before we begin, though, keep in mind that this is just a very brief overview of what's out there. We're only going to look at the most widely used products. To go into detail about everything would be impossible, because the world of specialized technology is huge and growing every day. There are so many devices and programs to choose from, I urge you to do some research and to work with your parents, teachers, counselors, and other professionals to decide what will work best for you.

TECHNOLOGY FOR PEOPLE WITH VISUAL OR LEARNING DISABILITIES

Earlier in this chapter, we talked about books and magazines in special formats—like Braille and audio recordings—for readers who have disabilities. But the bad news is, not everything is available in your favorite format. Thankfully, there are a lot of products that can help you gain access to the books, magazines, and other print sources that you'll need. Some are computer-based, and some are not.

If you do need a substitute for regular print, and if you have access to a computer, you'll find a vast library of information on the Internet. The problem is, especially for people with visual or learning disabilities, the same issues that make reading print an obstacle will also make reading the computer's monitor a challenge—unless you find the right software or hardware access solution.

The following sections discuss some of the access solutions for people who are blind, have low vision, or who have learning disabilities. Remember that this is just a very brief overview; we will also mention some specific products in passing, but you should not take this as an endorsement of one over another.

TECHNOLOGY FOR PEOPLE WHO HAVE VISUAL IMPAIRMENTS (BLINDNESS AND LOW VISION)

Reading Machines/OCR

Our first computerized reading aid, the reading machine, actually uses the power of the computer to read print aloud, or to turn the printed page into a computer file. Reading machines have been around for a long time. The person whose name is most often associated with this technology, Raymond Kurzweil, released his first reading machine decades ago, when computers were very big, and so expensive that only the wealthiest individuals could afford to own their own. Today, by adding a scanner to your computer, along with some specialized software referred to as Optical Character Recognition (OCR), you can turn your own computer into a machine that will read books, magazines, newspapers, and other printed material.

There are a number of reading machines/software programs currently available, and your school library might even have one on hand. Some of the more popular ones include:

Kurzweil 1000 (for people who are blind or who have low vision)— http://www.kurzweiledu.com/

Kurzweil 3000 (for people with learning disabilities)—http://www. kurzweiledu.com/

Vera stand-alone reading machine—http://www.freedomscientific.com/

OpenBook reading software—http://www.freedomscientific.com/

Screen Readers

Screen readers allow people who are blind, visually impaired, or have a learning disability to listen to the output of their computer. The screen-reading software works in conjunction with the computer's own sound card, or another voice synthesizer, to read the screen back to the user. Additionally, the "talking computer" will pronounce the keystrokes themselves as they are entered. For people who have very little or no vision, a screen reader is one of the most powerful computer access tools available. And for many who have learning disabilities, it has been shown that reading and listening at the same time can greatly increase speed and comprehension.

Some of these programs are very powerful and require a good deal of training. For this reason, it is an excellent idea to consult with a rehabilitation counselor, occupational therapist, or other professional before making a purchase.

Some of the most popular screen-reading programs include:

Hal—http://www.dolphinuk.co.uk

JAWS—http://www.freedomscientific.com/

Window-Eyes—http://www.gwmicro.com/

Screen Magnification

There are many more people who have a limited amount of vision than there are people who are completely blind. For this group, large print can be "just the ticket." Earlier, we talked about books in large print; while these are wonderful, there aren't many titles available. The ability to read large print on the computer's monitor can greatly increase the amount of information that can be used independently by people with a limited amount of vision.

There are two main ways that we use our computers: to receive information and to produce information. I have a slight visual impairment, and therefore I do all of my writing in 14- or 16-point type.

That means print looks like this on my computer's monitor as I work.

Once I have finished whatever it is I am doing, I simply change the whole thing back to 12-point type, and print it out. Unless, of course, I want to produce a large-print copy for myself! So, at the most basic level, your word processing program is a large-print program.

For people with different needs, there are a number of wonderful pro-grams that have many important options. Most allow the user to adjust screen magnification, change colors of the text and background, create "windows" that work like magnifying glasses to enlarge just certain por-tions of the screen, and much more. Some even provide large print in combination with speech output.

Like most of the other things discussed in this section, screen readers come with a very wide range of options and price tags. Consult with a professional to select the program that will work best for you.

Some of the most popular large-print computer programs include:

MAGic—http://www.synapseadaptive.com/

SuperNova—http://www.tiemanuk.co.uk/

ZoomText—http://www.aisquared.com/

Video Enlargers (CCTV)

We mentioned earlier that many important sources of information are not on the Internet. And most books and magazines are not and probably never will be available in Braille, in large print, or in a recorded format. Still, your ability to use the widest variety of media—including print—will be important for you in high school, in college, and beyond.

For people who use computer screen magnification—that is, people with varying degrees of vision—a CCTV (closed circuit television) can do much the same thing for print. The CCTV consists of a video display (basically a TV screen) and a camera mounted on a stand or, in some cases, handheld. Some CCTVs work together with a personal computer. Text appears on the monitor, and the reader can adjust text size, text and background color, and other features like brightness and intensity. These are quite easy to use and require practically no training.

Of all the devices and programs discussed in this section, the CCTV is probably the one that can be most often found in libraries and schools. If you'd like to see one in action, check with your local public librarian or ask your school librarian or counselors.

THE RESEARCH PROCESS

In high school, you'll be expected to do a wide variety of projects, and at some point, you'll probably write your first real research paper. This section discusses the "nuts and bolts" of research and the steps you should take to prepare a top-notch research paper.

WHAT IS A RESEARCH PAPER?

That sounds like a simple question, but actually, there are many types of research. *Webster's New Collegiate Dictionary* defines "research" as a "careful or diligent search." Many people do research without even knowing it. When faced with buying a new computer, for example, we might read reviews of various products and make our decisions based on these facts; we have, in this way, used research to guide us in our final decision.

In high school, you'll learn the basics of research and how to write a research paper. If you plan to continue your education after high school, you'll write many such papers, so getting the basics down will serve you well now, but might be even more important in the future. Follow the steps listed below, and you'll be well on your way to writing excellent term papers. And remember that writing is like a lot of things—the more you do it, the better you'll get and the more comfortable you'll become with the process.

Before You Start

Think of the steps you'll need to take, as well as how much time you should devote to each one. The first rule of thumb: Research usually takes longer than you anticipate. Make sure that you really understand the assignment. Are you supposed to use books, magazines, newspapers? Are you allowed to use Internet sites? How about footnotes and bibliography?

Choosing a Topic

A successful research paper starts with a well-thought-out idea. This seems like the easy part, but it is probably where beginners have the most trouble. When your teacher assigns a paper, he or she will most likely tell you how long (three to five pages, etc.) the paper should be, and this will affect the topic you choose. For example, in a five-page literature paper, you wouldn't try to talk about all of William Shakespeare's plays. In five pages, at best, you would write about one or two of his plays. Keep your topic manageable—not too broad, yet not too narrow—and you're on your way to writing a good paper.

In the early stages of research, don't be afraid to change your focus. You're learning as you read, and what you read may affect what you decide to write about. It might even change the way you think about your main topic. And while we're talking about topics, remember that, if you have a choice, choose to write about something you really care about. This makes the research process much more interesting, and your genuine interest will come through in the final paper.

Finding and Evaluating Information

Earlier, we saw that libraries are collections that are arranged in a way that makes them convenient to use. Get to know how your library is arranged. Your school library, your public library, maybe even your local college's library might be available to you. Getting comfortable with these libraries, and feeling confident in your ability to find information, is just the first step.

A big part of the research process involves judging, or evaluating, the information that you find. This skill is particularly important when you're using sources found on the Internet. How can you know if something is valid? Whether it is a brief article, a book, or an Internet site, you should look for an author's name and credentials. An anonymous posting on the Internet should be treated with caution and probably should not be used to support an argument or make a point. An article with a person's name, contact information, and some indication of expertise would obviously be preferred to one that lacks this information.

Organizing Information Effectively

Once you've selected books, articles, and other information sources for your research paper, the next step is to read them and to select those portions that you think you'll use in your final paper. Develop a plan, and then stick to it. As you read, if you encounter something that you want to include word-for-word, remember that you'll be quoting someone else's writing, and so you will have to give credit in the form of a footnote or an endnote. Keeping track of your sources will make the final project much less stressful; trying to backtrack and relocate something can take many hours—time that is better spent thinking, reading, and writing your paper!

You'll most likely get lots of guidance from your teachers as you undertake your first high school research papers. Remember that there is a lot of help available to you, from your teachers and from your school and public librarians. Librarians have a lot of training in how to find information—take advantage of that expertise, stay organized and focused in your work, and you might just find that writing a paper can be not only rewarding (in the form of a high grade), but also fun and stimulating!

USING THE INTERNET: SOME GOOD INTERNET SITES FOR CONDUCTING RESEARCH

Chances are, your school library has a Web site, and the librarian has likely selected some good Internet sites to link to. Check out your local public library's Web site, too. Here, you might find not only free sites, but also some very good subscription services that you wouldn't otherwise have access to.

The following list includes some general sites, most of which are available free of charge.

The Internet Public Library (http://www.ipl.org/)

The Internet Public Library is an excellent collection of very good links to quality resources. In addition to general reference sources, there is a special TeenSpace that offers links to "homework help," "clubs and organizations," and "colleges and careers."

The American Heritage Dictionary of the English Language (http://www.bartleby.com/61/)

More than 90,000 entries featuring 10,000 new words and senses. Most words have audio files that allow you to listen to the correct pronunciation of the term.

Biography.com (http://www.biography.com/)

This searchable database of more than 25,000 biographies of people, both living and dead, offers a "birthday search" that allows you to generate a list of people who share your birthday.

Encyclopedia Britannica (http://www.britannica.com/)

The Encyclopedia Britannica is a very well-respected, standard reference source that's been found in school and public libraries for decades. The electronic version, available by subscription, offers keyword searchability to this vast storehouse of information. Check out your school or public library's Web site to see if it is available to you. If not, you might want to consider subscribing to it yourself.

Information Please Almanac (http://www.infoplease.com)

How big is the nose on the Statue of Liberty? What's the capital of Wyoming? The Information Please Almanac provides short answers to factual questions like these.

Picture Searches (http://images.google.com)

The Internet provides access to many millions of pictures. If you need to view a picture of just about anything, you'll find it by searching the image section of the popular search engine Google.

After High School?

Cynthia Ann Bowman

The comprehensive secondary school encompasses two kinds of curriculum efforts and philosophies: one geared to the college bound and the other to work preparation. Although the majority of U.S. adolescents go to work rather than college, high schools usually fail to address the needs of these students, who graduate without the skills they require to be successful in the workplace. The guidance program is set up to aid the college bound, while vocational counseling and job placement services are neglected or nonexistent (American Association for Curriculum and Development, 1996). The secondary school curriculum seems more resistant to modification than the elementary school curriculum because high school is organized around subject areas and departments, much like a university. In such cultures, there is less attention to the needs of students, less collaboration, and often more competition for resources.

The effects can be measured in terms of student attitudes toward school. The National Center for Education Statistics (1995) reported that many secondary students characterize high school as having uncaring, inadequate teachers and unfair discipline. Dropouts reported their main reason for leaving school was that they did not like it. Schumaker and Deshler (1995) contend that enrollments of students with disabilities in regular secondary school classes continue to result in high rates of failure and dropping out, apparently for social reasons. Expecting regular classroom teachers to deal with the needs of students with disabilities by modification of the curriculum, space, and instructional methods will likely be a problem under traditional organizational arrangements. There are many avenues available to people with disabilities as they go through the transition from high school to the world of work. Training may be vocational, on-the-job opportunities, apprenticeships, or a trade and technical school. Through these programs, people in transition can obtain the job skills they need to secure employment. For those who are interested in more academic preparation for employment, community colleges, junior colleges, and four-year colleges and universities are valuable sources of education. The decision you make about what sort of training to pursue and what kind of institution to attend will depend upon your career interests, what type of job skills you have after leaving high school, and the nature and severity of your disability (http://www.NICHCY.org).

No matter what route you choose, there are many agencies available and willing to help you get where you want to be. While still in high school, talk to your counselor and special education teacher about what you would like to do. They can help you map out the steps to achieve your goal. Remember, even though you have a disability, you can be successful at finding a career that is right for you. If you decide that the path you wish to take does not lead to further education after high school, you still have many options to consider and opportunities to evaluate.

VOCATIONAL EDUCATION

Increasing numbers of secondary programs are adopting vocational models for students with disabilities. In spite of the trend, there is no clear evidence that such programs are particularly effective in getting good jobs for the majority of students. The vocational program resists becoming a dumping ground for academic castoffs, but only 30 percent of students who complete high school intend to go to college. There is a real sense of concern and urgency about improving vocational options in the secondary curriculum for all students because of the global economy.

Vocational success seems to be an implied promise of American education. All students are encouraged to remain in school with the expectation that on entering the workforce, their potential for earned income will have a direct positive relationship to the number of years spent in school. There is a relationship between employment and years in school, better than that between employment and academic achievement, but the ability to obtain and hold a job is more directly related to other factors. For many students, possession of a diploma merely assures entrance to more advanced training that will ultimately lead to employment. Many other students will receive virtually all training for an occupation from an employer after being hired. The diploma, therefore, is a device used to screen applicants, but it does not really represent any particular universal skills.

Skills in Vocational Education

The problem of students not acquiring sufficient skills has been considered by a number of groups and agencies. The common goals promoted by the U.S. Department of Labor for the Secretary's Commission on Achieving Necessary Skills (SCANS, 1991) have been used in vocational programs to address the needs of a new era. SCANS indicates that workers in the new economy must be able to do the following:

- Identify, organize, plan, and allocate resources—time, money, materials and facilities, and human resources.
- Work with others by participating as a team member, serving clients/customers, negotiating, and working with diversity.
- Acquire and use information.
- Work with and operate effectively within social organizations and technological systems.
- Work with a variety of technologies.
- Contribute to the development of reading, writing, listening, speaking, and mathematical systems.
- Contribute to the development of thinking creatively, making decisions, solving problems, and reasoning.

SCHOOL-TO-WORK TRANSITION

Due to the increasing demands for skills and the disappearance of high-paying, low-skilled jobs, the School-to-Work Opportunities Act of 1994 was passed to consolidate employment and training legislation grants for states. School-to-work is a new vision of vocational training for secondary schools that uses a comprehensive, community-wide effort to assist students in preparing for careers.

APPRENTICESHIPS

Drawing inspiration from Europe, primarily Germany, there are attempts to develop youth apprenticeship programs that offer relevant, work-based learning to non-college-bound youth. Unlike a work experience program, this plan intends to connect students to future employers, prepare high-skill jobs with a combination of courses and work experiences, and provide a full-time job at graduation.

There have been discussions in recent years about adopting a program of skill certification for high schools, a part of the reform movement that would put meaning into the diploma. In other words, in addition to a diploma, a student would earn a certificate specifying competencies he or she can offer an employer. This is essentially what happens in apprenticeship programs, but the employer is responsible for much of the skill training. However, because job skills change so rapidly, this is not very practical at the high school level.

Many jobs that are available today will disappear; many that will exist are yet unknown. It is clear that people who may be able to secure employment will need more technical skills. For students with disabilities, there is a danger that many will be technologically obsolete in the workforce. Jobs that many such persons now hold will be replaced by automation, and there will be competition for these positions from workers without disabilities.

The shifting nature of the workforce is a problem for vocational education, and the required equipment is expensive, then suddenly obsolete. Whereas American history courses or trigonometry will remain relatively unchanged, the latest vocational training uses equipment and software that will be out of date in a year or so. Technological changes can rapidly eliminate many jobs while creating demand for new ones, which causes the school to be out of step with the job market. Vocational education, therefore, must continuously change to meet shifting demands; this is difficult and expensive.

Another problem is that vocational education (and career education to some extent) is stigmatized by the types of students who have been placed in trade programs. Resnick and Wirtz (1996) reported that in 1990, students in vocational tracks took less course work in English, history, social studies, math, science, languages, and computer science than students in academic programs, and half of them took remedial mathematics.

The types of settings in which vocational programming may exist dictates what kinds of jobs will be included in the training efforts. Schools that are located in large, urban areas present different opportunities than those in smaller communities. The selection of vocational education models depends on demographic characteristics, commitment of the district to vocational education, available resources, and other factors. In general, there are high-cost training programs that require the investment of large sums of monies and personnel. The low-cost programs may be more easily offered, but may be of much less usefulness to students.

POSTSECONDARY TRANSITION

The Individuals with Disabilities Education Act (IDEA) mandates that each student have transition services included in the Individualized Education Program (IEP) no later than age 16, and planning notification of transfer to the majority must be made at age 14. IDEA requires transition services, meaning coordinated activities for a student, designed within an outcome-oriented process, to facilitate transition from school to post-school activities, such as postsecondary education, vocational training, integrated employment, supported employment, continuing and adult education, adult services, independent living, or community participation. The plan, known as an Individualized Transition Plan (ITP), is a separate component of the IEP.

Transition services are outcome-oriented to plan for the shift from school to postsecondary activities, including postsecondary education, vocational training, integrated employment, supported employment, continuing and adult education, adult services, independent living, or community participation. IDEA assures that this plan must take into account the student's preferences and interests. While it is true that most students, with or without disabilities, are fuzzy about their futures beyond high school, it is critical that plans be made for those with disabilities for many reasons. Traditionally, secondary schools have assumed little responsibility for the preparation of any student for anything but college. U.S. school systems have a curriculum geared to serving college-bound youth, this despite the fact that only about 30 percent of U.S. high school graduates matriculate to a four-year college. The remaining 70 percent enter the workforce.

Transition goals in the IEP should provide education programs that teach practical daily living and socialization skills, as well as academic skills. As students near the end of their public school careers, they should have annual goals and objectives related to career education, vocational preparation, and community living. As in other IEPs throughout the school years, the students and parents should be involved in goal setting. Although this may be particularly difficult for some parents, who look forward to school completion with a great deal of anxiety, it is nevertheless critical for them to have this knowledge about the student.

SCHOOL-TO-WORK OPPORTUNITIES ACT OF 1994

Probably because of an increased emphasis on academics and the fact that adolescents find vocational education to be socially unacceptable, this type of secondary training has been shrinking. Students are taking fewer vocational courses than in the early 1980s, there are fewer vocational teachers, fewer university programs training them, and fewer state employees work in vocational education. This trend continues, even though total secondary enrollments are growing and the vast majority of students do not intend to go to college.

In response to these trends, President Clinton signed the School-to-Work Opportunities Act on May 4, 1994, which authorized funding through 1999 to plan and develop school-to-work programs. The legislation (§ 2) noted that "three-fourths of high school students in the United States enter the work force without baccalaureate degrees," and many lack "the academic and entry-level occupational skills necessary to succeed in the changing United States workplace, which is changing in response to heightened international competition and new technologies."

Unemployment among U.S. youths is "intolerably high and earnings of high school graduates have been falling relative to earnings of individuals with more education." At the same time, "a substantial number of youths in the United States, especially disadvantaged students, students of diverse racial, ethnic, and cultural backgrounds, and students with disabilities, do not complete high school."

GOALS OF VOCATIONAL TRAINING

There will be many goals and objectives proposed for career education and for specific training. The diversity of the student population is such that broad goals should be stated for vocational training with more narrow goals and specific objectives identified for each student in the IEP and the ITP. The following goals are recommended for vocational training:

- Identify personal abilities.
- Develop individual areas of interest in accordance with abilities.
- Learn to compensate for personal limitations.
- Learn to control emotional responses.
- Develop an appropriate emotional repertoire.
- Develop a positive self-image.
- Develop acceptable standards of dress and appearance.
- Develop an awareness of social interactions.
- Understand motives and needs associated with the behaviors of others.
- Adjust behavior appropriately to different settings.
- Complete formal school with a diploma.
- Develop occupational awareness.
- Establish realistic occupational goals.
- Secure employment or develop short-term plans for employment after graduation.

INTEGRATION IN THE COMMUNITY

In 1987, the Center on Human Policy, Syracuse University (Research and Training Center on Community Integration, Center on Human Policy, Division of Special Education and Rehabilitation, School of Education, Syracuse University) issued a policy statement that has been used by many to guide planning and policy in the area of community living for adults with developmental disabilities. The major points include that adults with developmental disabilities should have:

- the opportunity to pursue the same range of lifestyles as nondisabled members of the community;

- the right and opportunity to live in typical, decent, safe, accessible, and integrated community housing;
- choices about the neighborhood they live in, the style of community housing, and the people with whom they will live;
- the same tenant and ownership rights and opportunities as other citizens, including the option to own or lease their own homes or apartments;
- the opportunity to live in housing free from the conflicting relationship of landlord and service provider;
- the opportunity to create a home of their own, reflective of their personal routines, values, and lifestyles;
- whatever personal assistance and supports they need to live fully in their own home and community with dignity, self-determination, and respect;
- the option to live in their own homes in the community without risking the loss of material or personal-assistance support;
- maximum control over their personal-assistance and other supports, with advocacy and support, independent of service agencies, in making these decisions;
- a right to determine who will provide personal assistance and supports;
- opportunities to be involved with ordinary people on a partnership basis and to develop relationships with neighbors, coworkers, and community members;
- decent, safe, and affordable housing, financial security to meet basic needs, health and medical care, and community transportation, employment, and recreation; and
- opportunities to contribute to the diversity and strength of communities.

COMMUNITY HOUSING

Amended after the passage of the Americans with Disabilities Act (ADA), the Fair Housing Act of 1988 requires that housing units be accessible to people with disabilities. In 1996, the U.S. Department of Justice filed its first suit in the U.S. District Court in Chicago, against an inaccessible condominium in Joliet, Illinois, after a woman using a wheelchair complained she could not find any accessible units there. Most people with disabilities live with their families or in independent living arrangements and do not receive formal residential services, a dramatic departure from 30 years ago, when many state institutions housed millions of Americans with disabilities. For example, of an estimated 7.2 million people with cognitive impairments, only 308,984 were receiving residential services as of 1993 (Mangan, Blake, Prouty & Lakin, 1994).

Various programs and activities may begin during school or shortly after graduation. These may be orientation experiences, career exploration, job training, employment evaluation, and special high school programming that is work related. There are many possibilities, each determined by local and state resources. Obviously, students residing in some urban communities will have a wider array of options than students in more rural areas. Nevertheless, there are several possibilities, and many of them are related to the various programs at the federal level. One of the most successful is cooperative education, a structured method of instruction whereby students alternate or parallel their high school or post-secondary studies, including required academic and vocational courses, with a job in a field related to their academic or occupational objectives.

Training at Employment Sites

Students develop skills for real jobs and learn appropriate work and social behaviors through interactions with coworkers that occur naturally in a work setting. There are many possible arrangements, like work-study, so those students can spend part of the day at school and part at work. Students who begin to work during school are much more likely to adjust to competitive employment when school is completed. Such experiences can prepare these individuals for eventual employment, and in many cases, lead to a permanent job where the student is already employed.

Job Skills Curriculum

Schools can offer instruction and practice in the skills necessary to obtain jobs using their existing vocational programs and/or special programming directed at students with particular needs. Special work-training programs have been developed in most high schools for many years, although vocational training has traditionally been for students without severe disabilities.

Supported Employment

Originally created to assist individuals with severe developmental disabilities, supported employment services (Rehabilitation Amendments of 1986, P.L. 99–506) are now available in every state for a wide range of clients. Because it was found that clients who entered sheltered workshops commonly never gained competitive employment, they are instead placed in a competitive employment setting at the outset, and learn work skills on the job. There is usually a high degree of involvement on the part of the client, who selects a job rather than being "matched" to one. The student and his or her family can work with the transition team to look for something that takes into account the student's interests, not just apparent skills or abilities. Skilled jobs and entry-level positions that have a chance for advancement can be more easily targeted. If the student is successfully integrated into the job, the chances for long-term employment are good. Support can include a job coach, trainer, and other considerations in an employment setting. In determining adjustment and satisfaction, the emphasis should not necessarily focus on wages; the living arrangement, family and social relations, and leisure activities should also be taken into account.

These should be considered in the transition plan and used as indicators of adjustment. It may be, for example, that those individuals with good jobs and fairly high wages may not be as happy or well adjusted as those who have good friends and a better quality of life as determined by other factors.

Small Business Administration

Some people with disabilities who are interested in going into business for themselves may qualify for federal assistance and low-cost loans from the Small Business Administration (SBA).

Employment Services

There are currently more than 2,000 local Employment Service (ES) offices located throughout the nation. A specific responsibility of this service is helping job seekers with disabilities; each office is required by law to have a specialist trained to work with these individuals.

Social Security

The Social Security Administration pays disability benefits under two programs: the Social Security Disability Insurance Program and the Supplemental Security Income (SSI) Program. The medical requirements for disability payments are the same under both programs and the same process determines a person's disability. While eligibility for Social Security disability is based on prior work under Social Security, SSI disability payments are made on the basis of financial need. And there are other differences in the eligibility rules for the two programs. Social Security Disability Insurance benefits may be paid to workers under age 65 who have disabilities. In this case, disability means a physical or mental impairment that prevents the applicant from working and which is expected to last for at least 12 months or to result in death. Students 18 or older who were disabled before age 22 also can receive monthly benefits when either parent becomes entitled to retirement payments or dies after having worked long enough under Social Security. Benefits continue as long as the condition prevents work.

SSI makes monthly payments to people who are aged, disabled, or blind and have limited income and resources (assets). To receive SSI payments for disability, the applicant must meet the Social Security definition of "disabled" or "blind." Also, to be eligible, the recipient must live in the United States or northern Mariana Islands; either be a U.S. citizen or in the United States legally; and, if disabled, must accept vocational rehabilitation services if offered. Individuals may be eligible for SSI if they have never worked. Those who receive SSI benefits can also qualify for Social Security if they are eligible.

Children and adults with disabilities may qualify for SSI payments. Eligibility is based on limited income and resources. States may add to SSI payments, and may also provide Medicaid, food stamps, and other services.

THE JOB TRAINING PARTNERSHIP ACT (JTPA)

The Job Training Partnership Act (JTPA), enacted in 1982 and amended in 1992, is the federal government's principal employment training program. The JTPA was created to prepare youth and unskilled adults for entry into the labor force and to afford job training to economically disadvantaged individuals and others facing serious barriers to productive employment because of special needs. Many individuals with disabilities meet the eligibility criteria. JTPA, administered by the Department of Labor, has a $4 billion annual budget, including the Job Corps, dislocated worker programs, and summer youth programs. JTPA is viewed as a relatively successful program because most of those who enroll in the program gain employment.

VOCATIONAL REHABILITATION

An agency in each state is responsible for the administration of vocational rehabilitation, supported employment, and independent living for individuals with disabilities. The Vocational Rehabilitation Program is designed to assist eligible persons with disabilities to achieve suitable employment, the Supported Employment Program works with individuals with severe disabilities who require ongoing support services to enter or maintain competitive employment, and the Independent Living Program is concerned with persons who have severe disabilities. The purpose is to provide them with independent living in the community and in the home. Services may include:

- medical, psychological, vocational, and other types of assessments to determine habilitation programming objectives and goals;
- counseling and guidance;
- referral for services from other agencies;
- physical and mental restoration services necessary to correct or substantially modify a physical or mental condition that is stable or slowly progressive;

- vocational and other types of training, including on-the-job instruction, trade schools, and training in institutions of higher education;
- interpreter and reader services;
- rehabilitation technology services;
- placement in suitable employment; and
- postemployment services necessary to maintain or regain suitable employment.

Similar to laws that apply to the school setting, federal law protects the rights and interests of the disabled in employment—the job application process, hiring, compensation, advancements, organized labor relations, training, and terminating employment. ADA stipulates that an employer cannot discriminate against a qualified individual with a disability, that the person with a disability be able to fulfill the essential functions of a particular job, and that the employer provide reasonable accommodations to assist in adjustment to employment.

Employers may not include unreasonable requirements nor unnecessary responsibilities and skills for a job. They are also required to make "reasonable accommodations" for employment access and job performance:

- Accessible and usable facilities
- Job restructuring, modification of work schedules
- Acquiring or modifying equipment (assistive devices)
- Modification of examinations for employment and advancement
- Training materials
- Provision of qualified readers or interpreters

CONCLUSION

No matter what your goals for the future include, there are multiple resources and pathways to help make them a reality. Much like Dr. David Hartman illustrated in his chapter "Sight and Insight," accomplishing your goals often requires a lot of hard work, a bit of stubbornness, and a passion to succeed. The sky is truly the limit.

REFERENCES

American Association for Curriculum and Development. (1996). School-to-Work Transition. *Education Issues*, an Infobrief Synopsis.
Copple, C., Kane, M., Matheson, N., Meltzer, A., Packer, A. & White, T. (1993). SCANS in the schools. In *Teaching the SCANS Competencies*. Washington, DC: U.S. Department of Labor.

Giangreco, M.F., Cloninger, C.J., & Iverson, V. (1993). *Choosing options and accommodations for children (COACH): A planning guide for inclusive education.* Baltimore, MD: Paul H. Brookes Publishing Company.

Government Accounting Office. (1992). *Labor issues: Report No. GAO/OCG-93-19TR.* U.S. General Accounting Office, Office of the Comptroller General, December 1992.

Learning Disabilities Association. (1992). *Inclusion: Position Paper of the Learning Disabilities Association.* Pittsburgh, PA: Learning Disabilities Association.

Mangan, T., Blake, E.M., Prouty, R.W., & Lakin, K.C. (1994). *Residential services for persons with mental retardation and related conditions: Status and trends through 1993.* Minneapolis: University of Minnesota Research and Training Center on Residential Services and Community Living, Institute on Community Integration.

McCarthy, M.M. (1994). Inclusion and the law: Recent judicial developments. *Research Bulletin, 13,* 1–4.

National Association of State Directors of Special Education. (1993). *The impact of inclusive school system initiatives on the education of students with disabilities.* Washington, DC: National Association of State Directors of Special Education.

National Center on Educational Outcomes. (1993). *Views on inclusion and testing accommodations for students with disabilities.* Minneapolis, MN: University of Minnesota College of Education.

National Center for Education Statistics. (1995). *Digest of education statistics.* Washington, DC: U.S. Department of Education, Office of Educational Research and Improvement, NCES 95-029.

National Center on Educational Restructuring and Inclusion (1994). *National Survey on Inclusive Education (Number 1).* New York: Graduate School and University Center, The City University of New York.

Office of Educational Research and Improvement. (1991). Delivering special education: Statistics and trends. Revised. *ERIC Digest.* Reston, VA: ERIC Clearinghouse on Handicapped and Gifted Children.

Resnick, L.B., & Wirtz, J.G. (eds.). (1996). *Linking school and work: Roles for standards and assessment.* San Francisco, CA: Jossey-Bass.

Schumaker, J.B., & Deshler, D.D. (1995). Secondary classes can be inclusive, too. *Educational Leadership. 52*(4), 50–52.

Secretary's Commission on Achieving Necessary Skills. (1991). *What work requires of schools.* Washington, DC: SCANS, U.S. Department of Labor.

U.S. Department of Education. (1999). Study of personnel needs in special education. Available online: http://www.spense.org.

———. (1995). *Individuals with Disabilities Education Act Amendments of 1995: Reauthorization of the Individuals with Disabilities Education Act (IDEA).* Washington, DC: Office of Special Education and Rehabilitative Services.

Curriculum and Disability: Pedagogical Considerations for Teachers

Cynthia Ann Bowman

Curriculum itself develops through the dynamic combination of action and reflection. Of special significance are the social relationships of the school—between teachers and students, the organization of classes, evidence of community, and opportunities for engagement.

In *Pedagogy of Freedom* (2000), Freire asserts that every student comes to the classroom with a unique set of characteristics and beliefs that cannot always be scientifically analyzed. Therefore, the teacher must recognize that each student is an individual and accordingly must be treated as such. The teacher has the responsibility for fostering this difference and acknowledging the varying beliefs and values the students hold. As human beings, we are all complex, and the nature of this complexity is why we cannot be held up to one specific standard. Respecting the individuality of students is the first step, and although some may argue against it, it is the most important move toward establishing a community of learners within the classroom.

Many students come to the classroom with the belief that their opinions will not be taken seriously. Some may be unwilling to speak up in class for fear that they will be put down either by their peers or by their teacher. Many, however, will discuss their lives and their communities if given the opportunity to do so in a safe and nonthreatening environment. Students who live with disabilities may acutely need to feel safe within the classroom. It is up to the teacher to be willing to discuss important issues that deal with students' everyday lives and to take that risk.

Why not discuss with the students the concrete reality of their lives and that aggressive reality in which violence is permanent and where people are much more familiar with death than with life? Why not establish an intimate connection between knowledge considered basic to any school curriculum and knowledge that is the fruit of the lived experiences of these students as individuals? (Freire, 2000, p. 36)

According to Maxine Greene (1995), each student will be on their own journey of discovery about themselves and life as they enter the classroom. It is the teacher's responsibility to instill within his or her students that they are all unique and distinctive individuals who will find their own ways of obtaining new knowledge. Not every student will learn or achieve in the same way; some will have talents in areas where others will not. By allowing students to share their own stories and hear the stories of others, they can learn to place value on differences; the ability to understand various perspectives will permit them to see the bigger picture. Students will no longer be able to simply focus on the color of someone's skin, the shape of their body, or a different means of communication; they will begin to search for a deeper and even a more spiritual connection.

Children differ genetically with respect to their intellectual proclivities. And because they do, the differences among them need to be taken into account in educational policy and practice. Each child in our schools should be given an opportunity to find a place in our educational sun. This means designing educational programs that enable children to play with their strengths, to pursue and explore those meaning systems for which they have special aptitudes or interests. (Eisner, 1998, p. 18)

IMPORTANCE OF BELONGING

A community possesses human interdependence, solidarity, a sense of culture and history, diversity and pluralism, and social integration. With the decline of a culture comes a loss of spirituality and aesthetic experience, which yields an emptiness, despair, and hopelessness. Perhaps that is one reason that people "surf the Web" and search for opportunities to reach out into cyberspace for understanding and conversation. Creating caring spaces requires that "classrooms should be places in which students can legitimately act on a rich variety of purposes, in which wonder and curiosity are alive, in which students and teachers live together and grow" (Noddings, 1992, p. 12). Caring, in community, does bring to education its greatest moral competence and worth. Education should be concerned about the whole person. Dewey (1916) said, "School should be a genuine form of active community life, instead of a place set apart in which to learn lessons" (p. 27).

Thomas Sergiovanni (1994) proposes that the most hopeful reform for education is to build community in the classroom, a partnership that allows for a shared learning experience and provides opportunities for personal relevance. Martin Buber's (1966) notion of community exists in the between of the *I/Thou* relationship and values dialogue, reciprocity, openness, concern for the relationship, and a rediscovery of the boundary between self and other. *I* is the beginning of dialogue; the *We* evolves through sacrifice, commitment to values, nurturing the bondedness, and time.

Man has always had his experiences as *I*, his experiences with others, and with himself; but it is as *We*, ever again as *We*, that he has constructed and developed a world out of his experiences . . . Man has always thought his thoughts as *I*, and as *I* he has transplanted his ideas into the firmament of the spirit, but as *We* he has ever raised them into being itself, in just that mode of existence that I call *"the between"* or *"betweenness."* (Buber, 1966, p. 107)

Buber's notion of the *We* affirms the individual and the community in much the same way Thomas Merton (1955) espouses that the essence of human life is one's connection to others. In Buber's words, "Only men who are capable of truly saying *Thou* to one another can truly say *We* with one another" (1972, p. 175). It is a slow progression, which awakens trust, belonging, and purpose—a process that cannot be forced. Indeed, one of the problems for community is maintaining a dual spirit of willingness to struggle for what one believes to be true while remaining open to another's perspective.

Minar and Greer (1969) view authenticity as a responsibility to self, an awareness of the person one ought to be, which creates a bond supporting the potential and growth of the other: "To be authentic is to establish integral connections with other people, nature, work, and ideas, thus making the world really one's own" (p. 72). Community nurtures the authenticity of the other, a relationship that allows for a shared learning experience, provides opportunities for personal relevance, makes meaning through narrative, lets go of control, and enhances caring.

WITHIN THE CLASSROOM

The ability to teach scientific/information literacy skills with text, voice, music, graphics, photos, animation, and video means that we can vastly expand the range of learning experiences, opening up the social and natural worlds of adolescents. All students can explore the relations among ideas and thus experience a more connected form of learning. Students can choose what to see and do, and they have media to record and extend what they learn.

What we consistently observe is the "otherness" that exists in every disability discussion. Students who become more involved in this discourse are usually those who have a friend or family member with a disability. Connections made to issues with which they have personal experience will lead to a deeper understanding of differences. For example, a colleague told this story:

I was close to an individual who was diagnosed as bipolar, and who committed suicide as a result of not finding help nor coping with his illness. The real tragedy is that his death could have been prevented. Sharing my story with my friends allows them to realize just how close to home emotional disorders really are.

Vygotsky (1978) suggests that deeper understandings, externally and socially regulated, become the basis for expertise. Discussion serves as a means to make an individual's thoughts accessible to others and to make the understanding explicit. An Ohio seventh-grader sent a letter to a local radio station, in which she asked for just one day when classmates didn't laugh or make fun of her limp and speech impairment resulting from cerebral palsy. A Nebraska middle school student was diagnosed with posttraumatic stress disorder after her classmates, one in particular, yelled at the teen, rammed her wheelchair into a wall, and mocked her. Providing opportunities to explain misunderstandings and clarify ideas is a necessary facet of building knowledge and a deeper consciousness and expertise. "Education implies not only the development of the individual's potential, but also the historical expression and growth of the human culture" (Bruner, 1987, pp. 1–2).

As Eisner asserts, in *The Kind of Schools We Need*,

Teachers cannot deal with abstractions or averages when they teach. Their knowledge of individuals is crucial in enabling them to make appropriate assignments, to provide comfort and support. . . . It is awareness of individual children that makes it possible for teachers to encourage the development of nascent but valuable interests and the expression of well-developed talents. (1998, p. 190)

Freire (2000) also reminds us that the curriculum cannot abstract itself from the sociocultural and economic conditions of its students, their families, and their communities:

It's impossible to talk of respect for students, for the dignity that is in the process of coming to be, for the identities that are in the process of construction, without taking into consideration the conditions in which they are living and the importance of the knowledge derived from life experience, which they bring with them to school. I can in no way underestimate such knowledge. Or what is worse, ridicule it. (p. 62)

Freire (1970) feels this kind of work is particularly appropriate for students whose voices have seldom been heard. As students begin to participate in this manner, their feelings of self-esteem increase. They begin to realize that their words and experiences merit a valuable place in their education, creating a continuous wave of connections and understanding. Therefore, educators must:

- help students understand their strengths,
- work with students to demonstrate those strengths, and
- establish patterns and strategies to maneuver around weaknesses so they are mitigated.

There are many possible approaches to curriculum design and instruction in schools. In each instance, however, the decision has to be made about how to include all students. Such factors should comprise the student's chronological age, rate of learning, academic goals, the family's and the student's preferences regarding academic instruction, and the need for skills other than academic. The focus is not how to help students fit into the existing curriculum, but how to adapt to meet the needs of any individual for whom the general education curriculum is inappropriate. In inclusive classrooms, curriculum takes on a major significance since, in the past, the principal reason for removing students was their inability to benefit from the general education program.

Especially at middle elementary grades and higher, the curriculum affects how integration can take place. Curriculum has to change if schools are to be inclusive of students with the full range of disabilities. For students with sensory and/or physical disabilities, the problem is how to access the general education curriculum; for students with cognitive disabilities, the problem is how to modify it. The instructional tasks of the teacher and the ability of students to profit from instruction depend on the quality of presentation and the capability of everyone to hear and understand. Many students who are disruptive, withdrawn, frustrated, or resigned to failure may be unable to see and hear clearly or may have problems understanding what is going on in the classroom.

ADVICE TO EDUCATORS

In addition to the many things that educators already do to foster a positive classroom environment, some of these ideas may be helpful:

- Build a strong, supportive social environment in your classroom.
- Set expectations for the student with special needs that are similar to those for all of the other students in your classroom (social, emotional, and behavioral).
- Appropriately discipline the student with special needs when necessary.
- Create a support system for the student at recess and lunch times, as well as for extracurricular activities (e.g., buddy system).

- Provide all students with opportunities for making choices throughout the day (e.g., games, group tasks, learning center activities).
- Provide for discussion circle times or regular class meetings so students can talk about feelings, concerns, ideas, and successes.
- Involve all students in problem solving.
- Pair students for some jobs so that assistance is available if needed.
- Find a role for all students in the class regardless of disabilities (e.g., a student who is unable to run a race could be timekeeper).
- Communicate positive attitudes toward students with disabilities through your own interactions, comments, and behavior.
- Recognize the successes of the student with disabilities as a contributing member of the class.

This is the kind of teaching that works regardless of social or economic factors. It means seeing all students as hope-filled human beings who are capable of success; valuing their outside-of-school community enough to become a part of it; and creating a safe community of learners, void of power plays or competition. It means seeing all students as experts at something, and viewing all knowledge as challengeable. It means being supportive, and malleable—willing to shape our work, our craft, to the needs of the ones we are crafting it for.

REFERENCES

Bruner, J. (1987). *Actual minds, possible worlds*. Cambridge, MA: Harvard University Press.

Buber, M. (1966). *The knowledge of man: A philosophy of the interhuman*. New York: Harper Publishers.

———. (1972). *Between man and man*. New York: Macmillan.

Dewey, J. (1916). *Democracy and education*. New York: The Free Press.

Eisner, E. (1998). *The kind of schools we need*. Portsmouth, NH: Heinemann.

Freire, P. (1970). *Pedagogy of the oppressed* (M.B. Ramos, trans.). New York: Herder & Herder.

———. (2000). *Pedagogy of freedom: Ethics, democracy, and civic courage*. New York: Rowman & Littlefield.

Greene, M. (1995). *Releasing the imagination*. San Francisco, CA: Jossey-Bass Publishers.

Merton, T. (1955). *No man is an island*. New York: Phoenix Press.

Minar and Greer. (1969). *The concept of community*. Chicago: Aldine Publishing.

Noddings, N. (1992). *The challenge to care in schools*. New York: Teacher's College Press.

Sergiovanni, T. (1994). *Building community in schools*. San Francisco, CA: Jossey-Bass.

Vygotsky, L. (1978). *Thought and language*. Cambridge, MA: MIT Press.

SECTION V

Advocacy for All

INTRODUCTION

Individuals with disabilities face a great deal of discrimination, and having a positive attitude about yourself is an important self-defense against such prejudice. However, another effective way to deal with obstacles is to be aware that they may lie ahead and be prepared to face them. Through the cumulative efforts of devoted educators, disability rights advocates, and countless people with disabilities, there are many rights that are guaranteed to students with disabilities. The centerpiece of these rights is the principle of inclusion, which promises that these young people will have an equal chance to participate in the classroom and in other school-related activities. Students with disabilities and their advocates can ensure that these rights are fully effective by carefully guarding them against infringements as a result of ignorance or malice.

Advocacy is an important way to make sure that these rights are protected and fulfilled. Students with disabilities can empower themselves to act as their own advocates by becoming aware of issues they will possibly face and being informed about their legal rights; however, parents, siblings, and friends should also assume the role of advocate whenever necessary. Further, all school personnel need to be aware of the rights of students with disabilities and work to ensure that they are fulfilled.

Issues of advocacy have been included in many of this book's preceding chapters. This section directly examines the importance of advocacy for the rights of students with disabilities and the differing roles that various people have taken in this regard. We offer strategies and goals of advocacy, discussing why it is so important, and what it can accomplish. In a very real sense, everyone has a role to play in supporting students with disabilities, and this section is intended to show how very important advocacy really is.

Following these final chapters are two appendices that are provided as references and tools for advocacy activities. These resources can help students with disabilities to better understand their own personal experiences, and they can also be used by the students to educate others about their disabilities. Appendix I is a list from the Web site of the National Dissemination Center for Children with Disabilities (http://www. nichcy. org), which offers a large number of books about a range of disabilities for children and young adults that realistically portray related issues. In addition to these selections, we have included other currently released books on disabilities. Appendix II is a list of advocacy and empowerment Web sites related to disability that are aimed at students. Though Web site content (and existence) can change without warning, at the time of this book's completion, the sites listed were available online resources aimed at helping students with disabilities.

I Don't Like the Term Disability

Cheryl

Consider using "differently abled" rather than "disabled." "Dis" is never good. . . . it is *dis*advantaged, *dis*couraged, *dis*missed; it's never positive. I have four children: My oldest son Glenn, who is 17, would be considered developmentally handicapped. My 14-year-old daughter Robyn is identified as having Attention Deficit Hyperactivity Disorder (ADHD), and she has struggled to learn to read, but now reads well above grade level and takes honors and college-placement classes. My 10-year-old son Reagan is identified as being gifted with a high IQ and exceptional reading skills (better than high school), but he functions low in math processes (not conceptual math). My six-year-old daughter Kennedy is the most amazing math child, has a foul temper, and will one day be an exceptional reader, but her handwriting is so poor she is being referred to an occupational therapist (OT).

Each of my children has some kind of limitation, but they each have a gift to balance that. Glenn has a great personality, can make screaming babies laugh, and has a great sense of humor. Robyn is intelligent, a long-distance runner, and loves toddlers . . . she is part of a youth ministry group that works with poor kids in Mexico. Reagan can build anything, read anything, and is an amazingly creative writer. Kennedy has informed us that she is gifted, probably in reading but definitely in math.

When I taught at a career center, I watched kids who could not read well or had never passed a high school math class build houses, fix cars, do activity therapy with seniors, teach toddlers to swim, draw blood, win districtwide competitions in those areas competing against "regularly abled" students, and complete their first year of college. I learned that all students LD (learn differently); the problem is that not all teachers teach differently and not all people think differently.

✑ An Important Lesson ✑

High School Student

When I was 10, a brain aneurysm burst inside my head. I was paralyzed on the left side of my body, but I soon learned to walk. I had to relearn how to dress, climb stairs, and cut food. My left hand never regained full movement; I cannot open it because the part of my brain that sends those signals was permanently damaged. So, I learned how to do pretty much everything with one hand.

At 16, I was also diagnosed with learning disabilities and nocturnal seizures. In high school, I got extra time on tests if I needed it. In my senior year, I had to take trigonometry, and the school counselors had a conference with my math teacher to tell him that because of my learning disabilities I needed extra time and a note card with formulas. He refused, saying that it would violate all of his principles as a teacher to allow me to use a note card on tests. I looked across the table at this teacher, the same one who taught my older sisters and lived a street away from me, and I felt wounded and attacked. The school administrators later told me that they could force him to give me the accommodations. I felt pressured from both sides and ended up dropping the class. The administrators didn't try to talk me out of it. I am sure they were just as relieved as I was. I couldn't handle the stress of making a teacher go against "his values," and I didn't understand then just how wrong the whole situation was.

Right now, my environment is fairly responsive to my needs. I have a keyboard that is designed for use with one hand hooked up to my computer, where I type my papers for school and e-mail. I cannot use any computer labs on campus, though. I take the bus when my leg gets tired from walking.

I hated it when people wanted to help me because our society makes it shameful not to be completely self-sufficient or to give that appearance. Consequently, I hid my disability from most, and never spoke up to receive services or help that I needed. I thought of myself as a burden. I was wrong.

Advocacy, Empowerment, and Inclusion: Equal Educational Opportunities for All

Paul T. Jaeger and Cynthia Ann Bowman

Manuel has a significant hearing impairment and, as a result, has had trouble in physical education (PE) classes when they play team sports. The noise and commotion make it hard for his hearing aids to help him discern what the other team members are saying to each other or to him. He continued to be frustrated in team games until he explained the problem to his PE teacher. The teacher realized that letting Manuel's classmates know about his hearing impairment would help them to understand him better, and perhaps they could figure out a way to make sure he was always a part of the team. The teacher asked Manuel to explain his situation to the other members of his class, and together they discussed possible solutions. Ultimately, they decided that someone on his team would always make sure he understood what was being said. This simple action has solved Manuel's problem of not being able to fully participate in team sports.

For individuals with disabilities, the notion of advocacy is tremendously important. To achieve the social standing and legal rights that they have now, people with disabilities have had to act as advocates for their own rights. Throughout history, however, social forces have generally worked against the notion of individuals defending their own rights, as the first section of this book demonstrates. The historical tendency to separate people with disabilities from the rest of society led to the establishment of residential institutions outside of the community (Wolfsenberger, 1969), which dominated the treatment of individuals with disabilities for so many years. Even today, society often tends to encourage family members to view someone with a disability as a dependent and, in certain ways, even encourages people with disabilities to act as dependents (Pfeiffer, 2000).

Simply having a disability does not make one disadvantaged, marginalized, or oppressed by society. A disability should no longer be seen as an impediment to a successful career and a fulfilling personal life. Many personally and professionally successful people—doctors, lawyers, educators, and business executives—have disabilities. Making people in society realize this fact is a key element of advocacy at this point; social perceptions too often revert to viewing individuals with disabilities as dependents. Personal success stories, however, can be very persuasive in overcoming such stereotypes.

There is power in an individual's accomplishments, and personal stories can have great ability to increase awareness and affect social change (Stewart, 2000). Leading astrophysicist Dr. Stephen Hawking, who himself has a disability, asserted: "The way for disabled people to be appreciated is to be successful. For the physically disabled, this means being smarter than the next guy. No one is going to be impressed if you are a Paralympic [Olympic-style games for athletes with disabilities] champ. You have to be outstanding in absolute terms" (Hain, 1997, p. 14). Dr. Hawking's words are exceptionally important on this point, and his own life has been a brilliant example of success on absolute terms. He is world-renowned for his groundbreaking research into the structure of the universe. He is one of the great minds in physics, regardless of the fact that he has a severe motor neuron disorder or that he uses a speech synthesizer and a wheelchair.

In order to have a truly positive impact on social attitudes, stories of personal success must represent meaningful accomplishments. Good examples include how a group of individuals with hearing impairments forced phone companies in the United States and Europe to change their policies to make phone lines accessible (Lang, 2000), or how individuals with a range of disabilities forced the implementation of the Rehabilitation Act through a series of protests across the United States (Jaeger & Bowman, 2002).

Too often, however, stories that are embraced by society represent token successes of individuals with disabilities, viewing minor events as inspirational. Clearly, not everyone in society has a biased or negative attitude about people with disabilities and, depending on personal background and understanding, social perceptions vary among individuals (Turnbull & Stowe, 2001). Just as nondisabled people have a wide range of understandings of what it means to have a disability, those with disabilities also have many perceptions of the term and of what it means to have a successful life. For our stories to have a greater effect on society and on others, we need to lead successful lives on our own terms. And one of the best ways to ensure success is to advocate for our own rights and choices.

Most people tend to have mixed feelings about their own disabilities. The disability makes some things harder and has certainly led to difficulties at times, but it has also played a part in shaping who you are. You can't run from it, no matter how much you might try. Like it or not, the disability is a part of who you are. For many people, however, that fact can be hard to accept. One author ironically questioned what it meant to accept his disability: "Celebrate it in song? Drink toasts to it in the bar? Talk endlessly about tragedy? Decry a poor quality of life? Limp bravely into the sunset giving inspiration to all other people?" (Pfeiffer, 2000, p. 98). As this author demonstrates, there can be many negative ways to handle having a disability. But there are many positive ways to make peace with a disability, as well. One of the most important parts about advocating for your own rights is being comfortable with your disability and the role it plays in your life.

Some people describe being an advocate for one's own rights as "self-determination." This concept in based on four key self-determining elements: (1) the freedom to plan one's own life, (2) the authority to control one's own personal business and activities, (3) the support that is needed in everyday life, and (4) acceptance in one's own community (Pennell, 2001). "From an awareness of personal needs, self-determined individuals choose goals, then doggedly pursue them. This involves asserting an individual's presence, making his or her needs known, evaluating progress toward meeting goals, adjusting performance and creating unique approaches to solve problems" (Martin & Marshall, 1995, p. 147). Basically, self-determination is an attitude one can adopt in the role as an advocate for oneself, and the ideas behind it may help you figure out where to focus your efforts and how to best achieve your goals.

School is one of the places where self-advocacy and self-determination are most important. As a student, you must be responsible for standing up for your own rights and making sure that your needs are being met. You certainly are not alone; parents, friends, teachers, and counselors are there to help you. However, the person who can best represent you and what you need to be successful in education is you.

Your disability will play a significant part in your education, and your classes should reflect awareness of your special needs. As one educator has noted, "We ought to be creating conditions in school that enable students to pursue what is distinctive about themselves; we ought to want them to retain their personal signatures, their particular ways of seeing things" (Eisner, 2000, p. 581). In *Pedagogy of Freedom* (2000), Freire asserts that every student comes to the classroom with a unique set of characteristics and beliefs that cannot always be scientifically analyzed. There is not a formula that can be plugged in for the teacher to determine what her students may need or what may benefit them in their learning. Therefore, he or she must recognize that each student is an individual and accordingly must be treated as such. The teacher has the responsibility for fostering this difference and acknowledging the varying beliefs and values the students hold. As human beings, we are all complex and the nature of this complexity (of which a disability is only a part) is why we cannot be held up to one specific standard.

Laws mandate that your classes and assignments take your disability into consideration. You also should make sure, however, that your curriculum helps you to understand your place in the world. "Curriculum design must integrate an awareness of the larger societal dynamics and life contexts in which the children live and will return" (Beyer & Apple, 1998, p. 258). We develop ourselves as individuals more fully when we see ourselves in the context of others and the larger world around us. "Self-interpretation occurs within a context of encounters within which our sense of our own identity is constituted partially from a sense of others, objects, and situations; there exists a conversation between ourselves and others out of which meaning is constituted" (Beyer & Apple, 1998, p. 392).

Acceptance of the differences in each individual is the key to respect. If the classroom is set up in the belief that everyone will have a chance to voice his/her opinion without the possibility of being mocked, then each student can open up and feel as though he or she is part of something wonderfully unique. Creating value and meaning in everything within the classroom will open up the possibilities for students to grow and begin their journey of continuous transformation. For students with disabilities, respect is especially important with regard to the way one is treated and communicated with. Habermas (1979) alludes to four conditions in creating a favorable environment for communication: Words need to be comprehensible; any misunderstandings should be clarified or illuminated. The speaker and the listener must show sincerity to each other. All the information given must support the communication, and, ultimately, the communication must be appropriate in relation to moral and ethical commitments. This implies the sense of caring for the educative interests of each individual student (Henderson & Hawthorne, 1995).

Foucault (1980) describes personal empowerment as, "individuals are the vehicles of power, not its points of application" (p. 98). Students with disabilities must work to ensure that they see themselves as a source of personal power and as a part of the community around them. Nietzsche (1992) espouses that our narratives about ourselves only have worth if we alone have formulated that narrative, accepting anyone else's version of ourselves makes us a failure as a human being. We can only talk about virtue and make ethical decisions within a community where our values can be formed and tested. The concept that our lives are inevitably tangled with those of others, and that we must learn about others in order for our own narratives to grow is key to advocacy.

When each individual has an opportunity to think about what they really want to accomplish in their life, ideas about how to achieve those goals begin to develop. A supportive community will create narratives together to help protect individual and shared interests in order to realize their full potential. Our authority needs to be established through our honesty, integrity, willingness to be approachable and to approach others, and to have respect for not only others, but ourselves. We need to be active, energetic advocates for ourselves, while not letting ourselves settle for anything less than what we can dream.

Regardless of whether you prefer to think of yourself as your own advocate or a self-determined individual, you must make sure that you are given the education you have a legal right to receive and the personal respect you deserve. As you journey through high school and beyond, always remember that you are your own best advocate. Many people can help you and support you, such as your family, friends, and teachers. These people are extremely important to you, and they can certainly act as advocates for your rights. However, no one is better qualified than you to decide what you can and want to do in your life. You best understand your disability and how it affects you, what your personal goals and aspirations are, what will make you feel happy and fulfilled, and how you would define a successful life.

REFERENCES

Beyer, L. & Apple, M. (1998). *The curriculum: Problems, politics, and possibilities* (2nd ed.). New York: State University of New York Press.

Eisner, E. (2000). *The kind of schools we need*. Portsmouth, NH: Heinemann.

Freire, P. (2000). *Pedagogy of freedom: Ethics, democracy, and civic courage.* New York: Rowman & Littlefield.

Foucault, M. (1980). *Power/knowledge: Selected interviews and other writings, 1972–1977.* New York: Pantheon.

Gadamer, H. (1979). *Truth and method.* (W. Glen-Doepel, trans.). London: Sheed and Ward.

Habermas, J. (1979). *Communication and the evolution of society.* Boston: Beacon Press.

Hain, H.B. (1997, October). Light years ahead: One-on-one with Stephen Hawking. *WE, 14.*

Henderson, J. & Hawthorne, R. (1995). *Transformative curriculum leadership.* New Jersey: Prentice Hall.

Jaeger, P.T. & Bowman, C.A. (2002). *Disability matters: Legal and pedagogical issues of disability in education.* Westport, CT: Bergin & Garvey/Praeger.

Lang, H.G. (2000). *A phone of our own: The deaf insurrection against Ma Bell.* Washington, DC: Gallaudet University Press.

Martin, J.E. & Marshall, I.H. (1995). ChoiceMaker: A comprehensive self-determination transition program. *Intervention in School and Clinic, 30,* 147–156.

Nietzsche, F.W. (1992). *Basic writings of Fredrich Nietzsche* (Modern Library Series). New York: Random House.

Pennell, R.L. (2001). Self-determination and self-advocacy: Shifting the power. *Journal of Disability Policy Studies, 11*(4), 223–227.

Pfeiffer, D. (2000). The disability paradigm. *Journal of Disability Policy Studies, 11*(2), 98–99.

Stewart, T.G. (2000). Government, politics, and disability policy. *Journal of Disability Policy Studies, 11*(2), 109–110.

Turnbull, H.R., Jr. & Stowe, M.J. (2001). Five models for thinking about disability: Implications for policy responses. *Journal of Disability Policy Studies, 12*(3), 198–205.

Wolfsenberger, W. (1969). The origin and nature of our institutional models. In R.B. Kugel & W. Wolfsenberger (Eds.), *Changing patterns in residential services for the mentally retarded* (pp. 59–171). Washington DC: President's Commission on Metal Retardation.

Appendix I: Suggested Readings Related to Disabilities

The National Dissemination Center for Children with Disabilities (formerly known as "NICHCY") is funded by the U.S. Department of Education Office of Special Education Programs. The organization's Web site (http://www.nichcy.org) offers a wide array of resources for students with disabilities. The following suggested readings were assembled by the National Dissemination Center for Children with Disabilities to provide resources for people with various disabilities. The list includes more titles than just those that would be appropriate for students in high school or who will soon begin high school. Titles aimed at younger readers may still be useful for teenagers, as some of them may be the best portrayal of a disability or may be helpful in educating others about your disability.

Depending on an individual's disability, age, and personal interests, only some of these readings may be of interest or appropriate. However, such suggested readings can help students with disabilities begin to find stories they can relate to. For more titles and information about these suggested readings, see the National Dissemination Center for Children with Disabilities Web site. You may also wish to check your school library or local public library to examine the relevant titles from this list.

ATTENTION DEFICIT HYPERACTIVITY DISORDER (ADHD)

Caffrey, J.A. (1997). *First star I see*. Fairport, NY: Verbal Images Press. (Grades 6–8)

Carpenter, P., Ford, M. & Horjus, P. (Illust.). (2000). *Sparky's excellent misadventures: My A.D.D. journal, by me (Sparky)*. Washington, DC: Magination Press. (Ages 5–11)

Corman, C.L. & Trevino, E. (1995). *Eukee the jumpy jumpy elephant*. Plantation, FL: Special Press. (Preschool–Grade 3)

Galvin, M. & Ferraro, S. (Illust.). (1995). *Otto learns about his medicine: A story about medicine for children with ADHD*. Washington, DC: Magination Press. (Ages 4–8)

Gordon, M. & Junco, J.H. (Illust.). (1992). *My brother's a world class pain: A sibling's guide to ADHD-hyperactivity*. DeWitt, NY: GSI. (Grades 4 and up)

Janover, C. (1997). *Zipper, the kid with ADHD*. Bethesda, MD: Woodbine House. (Grades 3–6)

Nemiroff, M.A., Annunziata, J. & Scott, M. (Illust.). (1998). *Help is on the way: A child's book about ADD*. Washington, DC: Magination Press. (Ages 5–9)

Shapiro, L.E. (1993). *Sometimes I drive my mom crazy, but I know she's crazy about me: A self-esteem book for ADHD children*. Secaucus, NJ: Childswork/Childsplay. (Ages 3–5)

Smith, M. (1997). *Pay attention, Slosh!* Morton Grove, IL: Albert Whitman. (Grades 3–5)

Zimmert, D. (2001). *Eddie enough!* Bethesda, MD: Woodbine. (Ages 5–10)

AUTISM

Amenta, C.A., III. (1992). *Russell is extra special: A book about autism for children*. Washington, DC: Magination Press. (Ages 4–8)

Branon, B. (1998). *Timesong*. Las Vegas, NV: Huntington Press. (Ages 7–12)

Katz, I., Ritvo, E. & Borowitz, F. (Illust.). (1993). *Joey and Sam*. West Hills, CA: Real Life Storybooks. (Grades K–6)

Landalf, H. & Rimland, M. (Illust.). (1998). *Secret night world of cats*. Lyme, NH: Smith & Kraus. (The illustrator of this book has autism.) (Grades K–3)

Messner, A.W. (1999). *Captain Tommy*. Arlington, TX: Future Horizons. (Grades 1–4)

Prizant, B.M. (Ed.). (1997). *In our own words: Stories by brothers and sisters of children with autism and PDD*. Fall River, MA: Adsum. (Ages 12 and up)

Simmons, K.L. (1996). *Little rainman*. Arlington, TX: Future Horizons. (Ages 4–8)

Sprecher, J. & Forrest, J. (Illust.). (1997). *Jeffrey and the despondent dragon*. Muskego, WI: Special Kids. (Grades K–4)

Thompson, M. (1996). *Andy and his yellow Frisbee*. Bethesda, MD: Woodbine House. (Grades K–5)

Wilson, R. (1999). *The legendary blobshocker*. Arlington, TX: Future Horizons. (Written and illustrated by a nine-year-old boy with autism.)

DOWN SYNDROME

Carter, A.R., Young, D. (Illust.) & Carter, C. (Illust.). (1997). *Big brother Dustin*. Morton Grove, IL: Albert Whitman. (Ages 4–8)

Carter, A.R., Young, D. (Photographer) & Carter, C. (Illust.). (1999). *Dustin's big school day*. Morton Grove, IL: Albert Whitman. (Ages 4–8)

Dodds, B. & Hunt, J. (Illust.). (1997). *My sister Annie*. Honesdale, PA: Boyds Mill Press. (Ages 9–12)

Fleming, V. (1993). *Be good to Eddie Lee*. New York, NY: Putnam. (Preschool–Grade 3)

Fox, P. (1997). *Radiance descending*. New York: DK Publishing. (Grades 5–7)

Rickert, J.E. & McGahan, P. (Photographer). (1999). *Apple tree surprise*. Bethesda, MD: Woodbine House. (Ages 3–7)

———. (1999). *Russ and the firehouse*. Bethesda, MD: Woodbine House. (Ages 3–7)

———. (2001). *Russ and the almost perfect day*. Bethesda, MD: Woodbine House. (Ages 3–7)

Stuve-Bodeen, S. (1998). *We'll paint the octopus red*. Bethesda, MD: Woodbine House. (Ages 3–7)

Testa, M. & Paterson, D. (1994). *Thumbs up, Rico!* Morton Grove, IL: Albert Whitman. (Grades 3–7)

HEARING IMPAIRMENT, INCLUDING DEAFNESS

Addabbo, C. (1998). *Dina the deaf dinosaur*. Stamford, CT: Hannacroix Creek. (The author of this book is deaf.) (Preschool–Grade 5)

Blatchford, C.H. (1995). *Nick's mission*. Minneapolis, MN: Lerner. (Ages 10–14)

Booth, B. & Lamarche, J. (1991). *Mandy*. New York: Lothrop. (Hearing impairment, Ages 5–9)

Hodges, C. & Yoder, D. (Illust.). (1995). *When I grow up*. Hollidaysburg, PA: Jason & Nordic. (Deafness, Grades K–4)

Lowell, G.R. & Brooks, K.S. (Illust.). (2000). *Elana's ears, or how I became the best big sister in the world*. Washington, DC: Magination Press. (Deafness, Ages 3–8)

Piper, D. (1996). *Jake's the name, sixth grade's the game*. Unionville, NY: Royal Fireworks Press. (Grades 5–8)

Shreve, S.R. (1993). *Gift of the girl who couldn't hear*. New York: William Morrow. (Grades 5 and up)

Slier, D. (1995). *Word signs*. Washington, DC: Gallaudet University Press. (Grades 4–8)

LEARNING DISABILITIES

Banks, J.T. (1995). *Egg-drop blues*. Boston, MA: Houghton Mifflin. (Dyslexia, Grades 3–6)

Griffith, J. (1997). *How dyslexic Benny became a star*. Dallas, TX: Yorktown Press. (Ages 9–15)

Janover, C. (2000). *How many days until tomorrow?* Bethesda, MD: Woodbine House. (Dyslexia, Grades 3–6)

Schlieper, A. (1994). *Best fight*. Morton Grove, IL: Albert Whitman. (Grades 3–7)

Smith, S.L. & Booz, B. (Illust.). (1994). *Different is not bad, different is the world: A book about disabilities*. Longmont, CO: Sopris West. (Grades 2–6)

Stern, J., Ben-Ami, U. & Chesworth, M. (Illust.). (1996). *Many ways to learn: Young people's guide to learning disabilities*. Washington, DC: Magination Press. (Ages 8–13)

MENTAL RETARDATION

Carrick, C. & Carrick, D. (Illust.). (1989). *Stay away from Simon!* Boston, MA: Houghton Mifflin. (Grades 3–6)

Mazer, H. (1998). *Wild kid*. New York: Simon & Schuster Children's. (Ages 10–14)

Pulver, R. & Wolf, E. (1999). *Way to go, Alex!* Morton Grove, IL: Albert Whitman. (Grades 2–5)

PHYSICAL DISABILITIES

Benton, H. (1996). *Whoa, Nellie!* Columbus, OH: Open Minds. (Part of the *Best Friends* series, which features Kathryn, a girl with a disability who uses a wheelchair.) (Ages 8–14)

Carter, A.R. & Carter, C.S. (Photographer.). (2000). *Stretching ourselves: Kids with cerebral palsy.* Morton Grove, IL: Albert Whitman. (Ages 5–9)

Heelan, J.R. (1998). *Making of my special hand: Madison's story.* Atlanta, GA: Peachtree. (This book is about the making of a prosthesis.) (Ages 4–8)

―――. (2000). *Rolling along: The story of Taylor and his wheelchair.* Atlanta, GA: Peachtree. (Story of a boy with cerebral palsy learning to use a wheelchair.) (Ages 6–10)

Holcomb, N. (1992). *Andy finds a turtle.* Hollisdayburg, PA: Jason & Nordic. (Preschool–Grade 2)

―――. (1992). *Andy opens wide.* Hollisdayburg, PA: Jason & Nordic. (Preschool–Grade 2)

―――. (1992). *Fair and square.* Hollisdayburg, PA: Jason & Nordic. (Preschool–Grade 2)

Loski, D. & Sniffen, L.M. (Illust.). (1995). *Dinosaur hill.* Boise, ID: Writers Press. (The main character has cerebral palsy and uses a wheelchair.) (Grades 3–8)

Moran, G. & Westcott, N.B. (1994). *Imagine me on a sit-ski.* Morton Grove, IL: Albert Whitman. (Using a wheelchair, Grades 2–5)

Myers, C. & Morgan, C. (Illust.). (1999). *Rolling along with Goldilocks and the three bears.* Bethesda, MD: Woodbine House. (Using a wheelchair, ages 3–7)

Tuitel, J., Lamson, S.E. & Sharp, D. (Illust.). (2000). *Searching the noonday trail.* Muskegon, MI: Cedar Tree. (Part of the Gun Lake Gang Adventure series, this book features a boy with cerebral palsy who uses a wheelchair. The coauthor, J. Tuitel, also has CP and uses a wheelchair.) (Ages 9–12)

Useman, S., Useman, E. & Pillo, C. (Illust.). (1999). *Tibby tried it.* Washington, DC: Magination Press. (About a bird who can't fly.) (Ages 3–8)

SERIOUS MEDICAL OR LIFE-THREATENING CONDITIONS

Girard, L.W. & Sims, B. (1990). *Alex, the kid with AIDS.* Morton Grove, IL: Albert Whitman. (Grades 2–5)

Hamilton, V. (1999). *Bluish.* New York: Blue Sky Press. (Leukemia and using a wheelchair, Grades 2–6)

Harshman, M. (1995). *The storm.* New York: Cobblehill/Dutton. (Using a wheelchair, Grades 2–6)

Katz, I. (1994). *Uncle Jimmy.* West Hills, CA: Real Life Storybooks. (AIDS, Grades K–6)

Mills, J.C. (1993). *Gentle willow: A story for children about dying.* Washington, DC: Magination Press. (Preschool–Grade 3)

Mills, J. & Chesworth, M. (Illust.). (1992). *Little Tree: A story for children with serious medical problems.* Washington, DC: Magination Press. (Amputation, Ages 4–8)

Slote, A. (1992). *Hang tough, Paul Mather.* New York: HarperCollins Children's. (About a 12-year-old pitcher with leukemia)

Verniero, J.C. & Flory, V. (Illust.). (1995). *You can call me Willy: A story for children about AIDS*. Washington, DC: Magination Press. (Ages 4–8)

SIBLING ISSUES

Fox, P. (1997). *Radiance descending*. New York: DK Publishing. (Down syndrome, Grades 5–7)

Gordon, M. & Junco, J.H. (Illust.). (1992). *My brother's a world class pain: A sibling's guide to ADHD-hyperactivity*. DeWitt, NY: GSI. (Grades 4 and up)

Lowell, G.R. & Brooks, K.S. (Illust.). (2000). *Elana's ears, or how I became the best big sister in the world*. Washington, DC: Magination Press. (Deafness, Ages 3–8)

Meyer, D.J. (Ed.). (1997). *Views from our shoes: Growing up with a brother or sister with special needs*. Bethesda, MD: Woodbine House. (Grades 3 and up)

Prizant, B.M. (Ed.). (1997). *In our own words: Stories by brothers and sisters of children with autism and PDD*. Fall River, MA: Adsum. (Ages 12 and up)

Thompson, M. (1992). *My brother Matthew*. Bethesda, MD: Woodbine House. (Disability in general, Grades K–5)

VISUAL IMPAIRMENT, INCLUDING BLINDNESS

Chamberlin, K. (1997). *Night search*. Hollisdayburg, PA: Jason & Nordic. (Also available in Braille.)

Day, S. & Morris, D. (Illust.). *Luna and the big blur*. Washington, DC: Magination Press. (Ages 4–8)

Gardner, S. & Spurlock, J. (Illust.). (1997). *Eagle Feather*. Boise, ID: Writers Press. (About a blind Native American boy in the mid-nineteenth century) (Ages 9–12)

Martin, B., Jr., Archambault, J. & Rand, T. (Illust.). (1995). *Knots on a counting rope*. New York: Henry Holt. (Preschool–Grade 2)

Schulman, A. (1997). *T.J.'s story: A book about a boy who is blind*. Minneapolis, MN: Lerner. (Ages 8–12)

Turk, R. (1998). *Doll on the top shelf*. Los Altos, CA: Owl's House Press. (Presented in text and Braille) (Grades K–3)

OTHER

Aldape, V.T. & Kossacoff, L.S. (Photographer). (1995). *Nicole's story: A book about a girl with juvenile rheumatoid arthritis*. Minneapolis, MN: Lerner. (Grades 3–8)

Buehrens, A. & Buehrens, C. (1991). *Adam and the magic marble: A magical adventure*. Duarte, CA: Hope Press. (Tourette syndrome and cerebral palsy, Grades K–10)

Carlisle, K. (1994). *Special raccoon: Helping a child learn about handicaps and love*. Far Hills, NJ: New Horizon. (Disability in general, Grades K–3)

Gosselin, K. (1996). *ZooAllergy: A fun story about allergy and asthma triggers*. Valley Park, MO: JayJo Books. (Asthma and allergy testing, Grades K–6)

———. (1997). *SPORTSercise!* Valley Park, MO: JayJo Books. (Exercise-induced asthma, Grades 3–7)

————. (1998). *ABCs of asthma: An asthma alphabet book for kids of all ages*. Valley
    Park, MO: JayJo Books. (Asthma, Grades K–5)
————. (1998). *Taking diabetes to school* (2nd ed.). Valley Park, MO: JayJo Books.
    (Diabetes, Grades K–5)
Klayman, G. (1996). *Our new baby needs special help: A coloring book for families
    whose new baby has problems*. Omaha, NE: Centering Corporation.
Koplow, L. & Velasquez, E. (Illust.). (1991). *Tanya and the Tobo man: A story for chil-
    dren entering therapy*. Washington, DC: Magination Press. (Written in both
    English and Spanish, Ages 4–8)
Maguire, A. (1995). *We're all special*. Santa Monica, CA: Portunus. (Disability in
    general, Preschool and up)
Mulder, L. & Friar, J.H. (Illust.). (1992). *Sarah and Puffle: A story for children about
    diabetes*. Washington, DC: Magination Press. (Diabetes, Ages 4–8)
Peacock, C.A., Gregory, A. & Gregory, K.C. (1998). *Sugar was my best food: Diabetes
    and me*. Morton Grove, IL: Albert Whitman. (Diabetes, Grades 3–8)
Roy, J.R. (1999). *Bed potatoes: An activity guide for kids who feel yukky, miserable, and
    just plain sick*. Saratoga Springs, NY: Activate Press. (Grades 2–6)
Snyder, H. & Beebe, S. (Illust.). (1998). *Elvin: The elephant who forgets*. Wake Forest,
    NC: L&A Publishing. (Traumatic brain injury, Grades K–5)
Williams, M. (1996). *Cool cats, calm kids: Relaxation and stress management for young
    people*. San Luis Obispo, CA: Impact. (Grades 2–7)

FURTHER SUGGESTED READINGS

Alexander, Bruce. (1995). *Blind justice*. Los Angeles: Berkley Publishing Group.
    The first in a series about Sir John Fielding, an eighteenth-century blind
    detective.
Alexander, Bruce. (1998). *Person or persons unknown*. Los Angeles: Berkley Pub-
    lishing Group. Another in the series about an eighteenth-century blind
    detective, Sir John Fielding. This time, he is investigating a series of grue-
    some murders committed in the Covent Garden area.
Ashton-Warner, Sylvia. (1966). *Greenstone*. New York: Simon & Schuster. A large,
    lively family in New Zealand consists of a crippled father, once a famous
    English poet, the teacher-mother who must be the breadwinner, their 12
    children, and their half-Maori grandchild, who is heiress to a fortune.
Brown, Christy. (1991). *Down all the days*. Portsmouth, NH: Heinemann. This is
    the tale of a family living on the edge of absolute poverty in a Dublin slum
    as seen through the eyes of a son made mute and unable to move on his
    own by a crippling condition.
Bjarnof, Karl. (1958). *The stars grow pale*. New York: Random House. This is the
    story of a boy in Copenhagen in the early 1900s coming to terms with his
    progressive blindness.
Blankenship, William D. (1981). *Brotherly love: A novel*. New York: Arbor House.
    Ben Ryder's life is threatened by the release of his twin brother from the
    insane asylum.
Christie, Agatha. (1991). *The clocks*. Demco Media. Hercule Poirot is called in when
    an unidentifiable man is found dead in a blind spinster's sitting room.

Cook, David. (1978). *Walter: A novel*. New York: Secker & Warburg. A story of the life of Walter, severely retarded from his birth in 1930.

Crews, Harry. (1976). *The gypsy's curse: A novel*. New York: Pocket Books. The story of the hates and loves of a group of deaf-mutes.

Dickens, Charles. (2000). *Barnaby Rudge*. New York: Classic Books. A mentally retarded son of a murderer is arrested as a leader of a mob of anti-Catholic rioters in the late eighteenth century. He is jailed and sentenced to death.

Frame, Janet. (1982). *Faces in the water*. George Braziller Publishing. The story of Istina Mavet's years in a mental hospital and her strange fears.

Greenan, Russell H. (1978). *Keepers*. St. Martin's Press. Richard Vaughn's political career is bright if he can keep his mad brother, Nigel, out of the public eye.

Greenberg, Joanne. (1984). *I never promised you a rose garden*. New York: Signet Books. The strange world of insanity is examined, as a young girl spends three years in a mental hospital.

Greenberg, Joanne. (1984). *In this sign*. New York: Owl Books. Two young lovers leave a home for the deaf, marry, and enter mainstream American life.

Greenberg, Joanne. (1989). *Of such small differences*. New York: Thorndike. A man who is blind from birth and deaf since age nine manages to make his way in the world. He falls in love with an aspiring actress who drives a van for the blind.

Hofmann, Gert. (1989). *The parable of the blind*. Fromm International. This novelist studies Brueghel's painting, the *Parable of the Blind*, and re-creates the imaginary masterpiece.

Hugo, Victor. (1996). *The hunchback of Notre Dame*. New York: Penguin. The classic tale of a deformed man who lives in the towers of Notre Dame Cathedral in Paris.

Humphrey, William. (1984). *The Ordways*. New York: Laurel. At a family gathering in Texas in the 1930s, many stories are told, beginning with the travels from Tennessee to Texas of Thomas Ordway, who was blinded in the Civil War.

Kay, Susan. (1993). *Phantom*. New York: Dell. Kay retells Gaston Leroux's classic, *Phantom of the Opera*. She constructs a complete biography of Erik, starting with his birth in France in 1831, his neglectful mother, and his running away to join the gypsies.

Kelley, William Melvin. (1996). *A drop of patience*. New York: HarperCollins. The story of a blind African American jazz musician from his childhood and studying to blow a horn, to his tragic marriage.

Kelman, James. (1994). *How late it was, how late*. New York: W.W. Norton. This winner of the 1994 Booker Prize is a story of human survival in a bureaucratic world. Sammy's string of bad luck only gets worse as he discovers that he is blind.

Kesey, Ken. (2003). *One flew over the cuckoo's nest: A novel*. New York: Penguin Books. Bromden, a deaf-mute inmate of a western mental hospital, tells of the Chronics, Acutes, and Vegetables, and of their domination by the starchy big nurse until the arrival of McMurphy. The warfare between these two brings new spirit to the patients, but tragedy to McMurphy.

Keyes, Daniel. (2004). *Flowers for Algernon*. New York: Harvest Books. Mentally retarded Charlie Gordon participates in an experiment that turns him into a genius, but only temporarily.

Kipling, Rudyard. (1936). *The light that failed*. New York: Doubleday. The story of a young man, a war correspondent and artist working in the Sudan. He returns to London and must paint in a race against time, as he is going blind due to a battle wound.

Lagerkvist, Pär. (1982). *The Holy Land*. New York: Random House. Tobias and his blind companion, Giovanni, are cast ashore by pirates and take shelter in ancient temple ruins.

Lessing, Doris May. (1971). *Briefing for a descent into Hell*. New York: Random House. A look into the fascinating world of a madman.

Lott, Bret. (2000). *Jewel: A novel*. Demco Media. A Mississippi family is changed forever by the birth of a child with Down syndrome.

Marsden, John. (1988). *So much to tell you*. New York: Scholastic. Sent to a hospital by her mother, Marina, a disfigured Australian girl who refuses to speak, reveals her thoughts and feelings in a diary.

Mayerson, Evelyn Wilde. (1979). *Sanjo*. New York: Lippincott. A mother's stroke raises a father's concern about putting their 34-year-old Down syndrome daughter, Sanjo, into an institution.

McCullers, Carson. (1983). *The heart is a lonely hunter*. New York: Bantam Books. In a southern town, a mute becomes the recipient of the confidences of several residents.

McMahon, Thomas A. (2003). *Loving little Egypt*. Chicago: University of Chicago Press. A nearly blind man in the 1920s discovers how to make free telephone calls worldwide and is hunted down by the authorities.

Page, Jake. (1993). *The stolen gods*. New York: Ballantine. Another adventure of the blind artist/sleuth, Mo Bowdre. Ancient Hopi rituals, modern-day tribal life, and rough and tough crooks combine into a clever and complicated plot.

Percy, Walker. (1981). *The second coming*. New York: Pocket Books. Will Barrett moves to the North to relieve his feelings of dislocation in his native South, only to feel equally homeless and aimless. He falls in love with a dancer and moves back to the South, but all the while he is still plagued by the secrets of his youth.

Richards, Judith. (1981). *The sounds of silence*. New York: Pocket Books. After returning home, Aramenta Lee discovers that her son, who she thought was stillborn 30 years ago, is a deaf-mute recluse raised in a basement by her crazy mother.

Safire, William. (1977). *Full disclosure: A novel*. New York: Doubleday. While meeting with leaders in Russia, the president is blinded by an assassin's bullet. He must learn to cope not only with the international crisis, but also with pressure at home to resign, while trying to adjust to his blindness.

Saramago, José. (1998). *Blindness*. New York: Harcourt. One by one, people are being struck blind. The government quarantines them under armed guard, but the disease keeps spreading. A hierarchy of terror arises among them as more and more blind arrive. This book shows how vulnerable humans are, and how blind.

Stewart, Michael. (1988). *Blindsight*. St. Martin's Press. A young boy tries to prevent his blind father from ever seeing again.

Stone, Katherine. (1998). *Imagine love*. New York: Random House. When Cole Taylor returns to his childhood sweetheart, Claire, and discovers she has gone blind, they move to London together. Claire meets her pen pal, Lady Sarah Pembroke, who is being stalked by a serial killer.

West, Paul. (1993). *Love's mansion*. Overlook Press. Childhood sweethearts find their lives changed when the young man returns blinded from the First World War.

Yankowitz, Susan. (1976). *Silent witness*. New York: Random House. Anna, deaf and dumb, is accused of murdering her lover. How she finds her true identity is the story of this powerful novel.

Appendix II: Online Resources for Students with Disabilities

The DRM WebWatcher Just for Kids: http://www.disabilityresources.org/ KIDS.html. Sites for, by, and about kids and teens with disabilities and chronic illnesses.

Band-Aids and Blackboards: Teens: http://www.faculty.fairfield.edu/fleitas/ contteen.html. A site about growing up with medical problems.

Ability OnLine Support Network: http://www.ablelink.org/public/default.htm. "An electronic mail system that connects young people with disabilities or chronic illnesses to disabled and nondisabled peers and mentors." Provides information, educational strategies, employment opportunities, peer support, and a list of links to Web sites about chronic illness.

Kids as Self-Advocates (KASA): http://www.fvkasa.org/. Youth with special health-care needs speaking on behalf of themselves.

Encourage Online: http://www.encourageonline.org/. A place for teens with chronic illness and their family and friends to talk, connect, and have fun with someone who understands.

Winners on Wheels (WOW) Online: http://www.wowusa.com/. WOW empowers kids in wheelchairs by encouraging personal achievement through creative learning and expanded life experiences that lead to independent living skills.

Teens with Crohn's Disease Web Site: http://www.pages.prodigy.net/mattgreen. A place for teens/by teens with Crohn's disease to share stories and information.

@ctiveTeen: http://www.disabilitycentral.com/activteen/index.html. An e-zine written by and for teens with disabilities. Includes a chat room, message boards, game room, advice, and University of Hard Knocks.

Office of Employment Support Program, Youth with Disabilities, Social Security Administration: http://www.ssa.gov/work/Youth/youth2.html. This section of the larger *The Work* site is dedicated to youth with disabilities, their parents and families, teachers, and counselors.

Starbright Foundation: http://www.starbright.org/. A computer network where hospitalized children and teens can interact with a community of peers and help each other cope with the day-to-day realities of living with illness.

Common Thread: http://www.commonthread.org/home.html. This Web community is for young people with illness and disability in their lives as patients, siblings, or friends.

Bright Futures Encounter Forms for Families: http://www.brightfutures.org/ encounter/family/index.html. Encounter forms are used to record information and questions before a visit to a health-care provider. The "Ages 6 Years–Adolescence" section has forms for teens.

Teen Chronic Illness Resources: http://www.dartmouth.edu/dms/koop/resources/ chronic_illness/chronic.shtml. Biographies of teens with chronic illness developed by a student at Dartmouth University. Links include diagnosis-specific sites and other online support for teens with chronic illnesses.

The Under 21 Page: http://www.silcom.com/~sblc/under21.html. Especially for children and teens with rheumatic diseases and parents, family, friends, and health professionals wanting to learn more.

LD Online: Kid Zone: http://www.ldonline.org/kidzone/kidzone.html. For children and teens with learning disabilities; includes their stories, articles, and artwork.

National Youth Leadership Network: http://www.nyln.org. The National Youth Leadership Network (NYLN) is dedicated to advancing the next generation of disability leaders.

http://www.4girls.gov/fit/disabilities.htm.

http://www.kidshealth.org/.

http://www.ldonline.org/.

AHEAD—Association on Higher Education and Disabilities: http://www.ahead.org.

Council for Exceptional Children: http://www.cec.sped.org/.

Internet Resources for Special Children: http://www.irsc.org/.

NTA—National Transition Alliance for Youth and Disabilities: http://www.dssc.org/ nta/.

Parents Helping Parents: http://www.php.com/.

Assistive Technologies: http://www.lti.cs.cmu.edu/scs; http://www.soeweb. ssyr.edu; http://www.ataccess.org/; http://www.assistivetech.com/; http://www.closingthegap.com/; http://www.at-center.com.

Complete Disability Network: http://www.members.aol.com/.

Financial Aid for Students with Disabilities: http://www.finaid.org/finaid/ documents/heath.html.

NASP—National Association of School Psychologists: http://www.naspweb.org/.

National Academy for Child Development: http://www.nacd.org/.

National Organization for Rare Diseases: http://www.rarediseases.org/.

PACER Center: http://www.pacer.org/.

Parents Place: http://www.parentsplace.com/.

Yahoo! Special Education: http://www.dir.yahoo.com/education/special_education/.

Index

Adolescent(s), with disabilities
  dating considerations for, 70–82
  friendship development in, 71–72
  interpersonal communication
    among, 72–74
  romantic involvement in, 72
  self-esteem issues of, 75–76
  sexual knowledge of, 76–78
Advocate(s), 103–104
American Heritage Dictionary of the
  English Language, 131
Americans with Disabilities Act
  (ADA), 7, 29, 30, 138
Apprenticeships, 134–135
"Arc's Self-Advocacy Activities,
  The," 103
As I Am, 74
Asperger's syndrome, 88
Attention deficit hyperactivity
  disorder (ADHD), 161–162
Autism, 37, 162
Autobiography of a Face, The, 53

Babbitt, Raymond, 39, 43
Bacon, Francis, 48–49
Beattie v. Board of Education of City
  of Antigo, 51
Becoming DateSmart, 79
Bell, Alexander Graham, 10
Belonging, importance of, 145–146
Benefactor relationships, 42
Best friends, 41–42

Black Stork, The, 11
Blind persons, 126–128
Blindness, 165
Bond, Thomas, 10
Bondi, J., 91
Bowman, C.A., 72, 172
Braille, Louis, 10
Braille materials, 121–122
Bramble, K., 70
Brown v. Board of Education, 8
Buber, M., 146

Califano, Joseph, 14
Calvin, John, 9, 49
Cancer, 27
Center on Human Policy, Syracuse
  University, 137
Champagne, Marklyn P., 79
Cherry v. Matthews, 14
Children, 41–42, 43
Children of a Lesser God, 51–52
Circles, 79
Classroom, 146–148
  environment of, 109–113
  instruction in, 112
  life inside, 59–60
  life outside, 60–61
Clinton, William, 136
Closed circuit television
  (CCTV), 128
Code of Justinian, 8–9, 49
Communication, 72–74

Community(ies)
of advocates, 103–104
integration into, 137–138
reaching out to, 104
Community housing, 138–141
Council for Exceptional
Children (CEC), 5
Crane, Stephen, 50–51
Credulity, 40
Cruise, Tom, 37
Culture
disabilities as, 32–34
disabilities in, 28–32
Cure, The, 72
Curriculum, 108–116
advice for students, 114–116
defined, 108
and disability, 144–149
high school, 108–109
individualized learning situations,
113

Darwin, Charles, 11
Dating considerations, 70–82
Deaf parents, 25
Deafness, 163
Department of Health, Education, and
Welfare, 14, 19
Deshler, D.D., 132
Dewey Decimal Classification
(DDC), 119–120
Dewey, J., 145
DiCaprio, Leonardo, 37
Disabilities Education Act, 52
Disability(ies), 153
adolescents with, dating
considerations for, 70–82
cancer, 27
as culture, 32–34
in culture, 28–32
curriculum and, 144–149
in feature films, 38–43
high school students with,
experiences of, 87–88
integration, education, and struggle
for legal rights, 7–19
juvenile rheumatoid arthritis, 26
in literature, images of, 45–56

persons with
case examples, 25–27
library materials for, 121–124
technology for, 125–128
treatment of, 8–13
physical, 164
public perception of, 36–44
students with
access as barrier to, 66–69
community of advocates for,
103–104
electives for, 66
extracurricular activities and, 66–69
managing educational supports
for, 98–107
online resources for, 170–171
reaching out to community
for, 104
required courses for, 66
self-determination of, 104–105
suggested readings related to,
161–169
teacher with, 3–6
Disability rights protests, 13–15
Dominique and Eugene, 41–42
Down syndrome, 162–163
Dream(s), envisioning of, 64–65
Dyslexia, 87

Education
in integrated environment,
importance of, 7–8
for persons with disabilities, 7–19
sex, 76
special, 61–62
vocational, 133–134
Education for All Handicapped
Children Act (EAHCA), 15
Educational supports, 98–107
Educator(s), advice to, 148–149
Eisner, E., 147
Elliott, J.E., 93–94
Encyclopedia Britannica, 131
Environment, integrated, 7–8. *See also*
Classroom, environment of
Equal educational opportunities,
155–160
Extracurricular activities, 66–69

Family, 42
Faulkner, William, 51
Field, S., 104
Film(s), disabilities in, 36–44
Ford, Gerald, 13–14
Forrest Gump, 42, 43
Foundation for Child Welfare, 11
Franklin, Benjamin, 10
Freak the Mighty, 52
Free appropriate public education
    (FAPE), 15–19
    in transition to high school, 94–95
Freire, P., 144, 147, 157
Friend(s), nondisabled, 43
Friendship, 71–72

Gallaudet College, 52
Galton, Sir Francis, 11, 51
Gettysburg College, 64
Gilman, Charlotte Perkins, 50
Gordon, P.A., 72, 173
Grading, 113
Graduation, high school, 93–94
Grealy, Lucy, 53
Greene, M., 145
Greer, 146
Gullibility, 40

Habermas, J., 158
Hall(s), navigation of, 93
Hall, Edward, 48
Hansen's disease, 49
Hapner, A., 105
Hearing impairment, 163
*Hereditary Genius: An Inquiry into Its
    Laws and Consequences*, 11
High school
    campus of, in transition to high
        school, 92–93
    curriculum of, described, 108–109
    life after, 132–143
        apprenticeships, 134–135
        community housing, 138–141
        employment services, 140
        integration in community, 137–138
        job skills curriculum, 139
        postsecondary transition, 135–136
        SBA, 140

School-to-Work Opportunities Act
    of 1994, 136–137
    school-to-work transition, 134
    Social Security, 140–141
    supported employment, 139–140
    training at employment sites, 139
    vocational training, goals of, 137
middle school *vs.*, 91–92
transition to, 89–97
    FAPE in, 94–95
    graduation requirements in, 93–94
    instructional accommodations
        in, 95–96
    introduction to, 89
    navigating halls in, 93
    planning meeting for, 90–91
    recommendations in, 96
    size of campus in, 92–93
    student orientation in, 92
    support services in, 94–95
High school students, disabilities in,
    experiences of, 87–88
Hoffman, A., 104
Hoffman, Dustin, 37
Holinshed, Raphael, 48

I Am Sam, 43
Imel, B., 105
Inclusion, meaning of, 3–6
Independent Living Program, 141
Individualized Education Programs
    (IEPs), 5, 17, 66, 90, 91, 95, 96, 98, 99,
    135–136
    meetings of, leading of, 105–106
Individualized Transition Plan (ITP), 136
Individuals with Disabilities Education
    Act (IDEA), 15–19, 29, 89–90, 135
Information Please Almanac, 131
Inspiration station, defined, 93
Institute for Community Inclusion, 104
Integrated environment, 7–8
Integration, 7–19
Internet, 130–131
Internet Public Library, 131
Interpersonal communication, 72–74
Intimate relationships, 42
Itard, Jean-Marc-Gaspard, 10
Izzy, Willy-Nilly, 72

Joan of Arcadia, 44
Job Training Partnership Act
    (JTPA), 141
Justinian, 49
Juvenile rheumatoid arthritis, 26

Keller, Helen, 10–11, 45–46
Kewman, D., 75
Kind of Schools We Need, The, 147
Komensky, Jan Amos, 10

Large print publications, 122–123
Learning disabilities
    in high school students, 87
    suggested readings related
        to, 163
    technology for people with, 126
Learning models, 113–114
Least restrictive environment
    (LRE), 17–18
Legal rights, struggle for, 7–19
Leprosy, 49
Library(ies), 118–121
Library of Congress, 124, 125
Life Facts, 80
Life Horizons, 79–80
Life-threatening conditions,
    164–165
Lincoln, Abraham, 52
Luther, Martin, 9, 49

Mather, Cotton, 9–10
Matthews, David, 14
Matthews v. Cherry, 8
McGahey-Kovac, M., 105
Medical conditions, 164–165
Medoff, M., 51–52
Mental retardation, 163
Merton, T., 146
Middle school, 91–92
Mills v. Board of Education, 8, 13
Milton, 49–50
Minar, 146
Monster, The, 50–51
Monsters, 38–39
Montaigne, 47–48
More, Sir Thomas, 48
My Body Is Not Who I Am, 75

National Center for Education
    Statistics, 132
National Dissemination Center
    for Children with Disabilities,
    152, 161
National Information Center for
    Children and Youth with Disabilities
    (NICHCY), 79, 161
National Information Center for
    Handicapped Children and Youth
    Web site, 100
National Library Service for the
    Blind and Physically Handicapped
    (NLS), 124–125
Nelson, Philip, 9, 10, 19
Nixon, Richard, 13, 15
Note taking, 112–113
Notting Hill, 44

Oedipus Rex, 47
Of a Monstrous Child, 47–48
Of Deformity, 48–49
Of Mice and Men, 38, 39, 40, 42
On His Blindness, 49–50
Online resources, 170–171
Optical Character Recognition
    (OCR), 126
Orientation, in transition to high
    school, 92
Other Sister, The, 43
Outreach Education, 102
Overbrook School for the Blind, 59

*PARC v. Commonwealth of
    Pennsylvania*, 8
Parent Teacher Student Organization
    (PTSO), 37
Partner(s), attracting of, 74–75
Pedagogy of Freedom, 144, 157
Peer relationships, 41
*Pennsylvania Association for Retarded
    Children (PARC) v. Commonwealth of
    Pennsylvania*, 13
Person-first language, 28–29
Philbrick, R., 52
Planned Parenthood Federation
    of America and Teens
    Health, 78

Planned Parenthood Federation of
    America Peer Education Programs
    for Teens, 77
Ponce de Leon, Pedro, 10
Public schools, life in, 59–65

Rain Man, 37, 39, 41, 43
Reading machines, 126–128
"Recording for the Blind," 123
"Recording for the Blind and Dyslexic"
    (RFB&D), 123, 124
Reeve, Christopher, 74
Rehabilitation Act, 13, 14, 15, 29, 30
Research papers, 128–131
Research process, 128–131
Resnick, L.R., 135
Richard III, 46, 48
Roman law, 49
Romantic involvement, 72

School(s)
    public, 59–65
    within a school, for students with
        disabilities, 114
    year-round, for students with
        disabilities, 114
School-to-Work Opportunities
    Act of 1994, 134, 136–137
School-to-work transition, 134
Schumaker, J.B., 132
Science of Life, The, 12
Screen magnification, 127–128
Secretary's Commission on
    Achieving Necessary Skills
    (SCANS), 134
Segregation, 37–38
Self-determination, 104–105
Self-esteem, 75–76
Sergiovanni, T., 145
Sex education, 76, 79–80
Sexual knowledge, 76–78
Shakespeare, William, 46, 48
Sibling issues, 165
Simple Plan, A, 40
Sling Blade, 38, 39, 41
Small Business Administration
    (SBA), 140
Social Security Administration, 140–141

Social Security Disability Insurance
    Program, 140
Somebody Somewhere, 104
Sophocles, 47
Sound and the Fury, The, 51
Special education, 61–62
Stanfield, James, 78
"Steps to Self-Determination"
    curriculum, 104
Student(s), with disabilities
    extracurricular activities and, 66–69
    managing educational supports
        for, 98–107
Student-centered learning models,
    113–114
Student's Guide to the IEP, A, 105
Supplemental Security Income (SSI)
    program, 140
Support services, 94–95
Supported Employment Program,
    141–142

Talking books, 123
Tate, Carla, 43
Teacher(s), pedagogical considerations
    for, 144–149
There's Something about Mary, 40
Thurlow, M.L., 93–94
Tim, 42, 43
To Kill a Mockingbird, 38–39
Tourette's syndrome, 88
Towards Intimacy, 75
Tracking, 63–64
Transition to high school, 89–97.
    See also High school, transition to

University of Washington, 11

Video(s), general, 80
Video enlargers (CCTV), 128
Vision problems, 88, 126–128, 165
Vocational education, 133–134
Vocational rehabilitation, 141–142
Vocational Rehabilitation Program,
    141–142
Vocational training, goals of, 137
Voigt, Cynthia, 72
Vygotsky, L., 147

Walker-Hirsch, Leslie, 79
Watson v. City of Cambridge, 51
Webster's Dictionary, 89
Webster's New Collegiate Dictionary, 129
West Wing, 44
What's Eating Gilbert Grape?, 37, 39–40,
    41, 42
Wiles, J., 91
Williams, D., 104
Wirtz, J.G., 135

Without Pity, 74
Withstanding Ovation, 76
World Wide Web (WWW), 104

Yeager, N., 110
Year-round schooling, 114
Yellow Wallpaper, The, 50
Ysseldyke, J.E., 93–94

"Zero-reject" situation, 19

About the Editors
and Contributors

RHONDA S. BLACK is an associate professor at the University of Hawaii at Manoa in the Department of Special Education. Her research interests include the use of narrative to promote reflection in teacher education students; transition from school to adult living for individuals with disabilities; and social competence and community integration of individuals with disabilities. Her work has appeared in *Action in Teacher Education, Teacher Education and Special Education, Remedial and Special Education, Education and Training in Mental Retardation and Developmental Disabilities, Disability Studies Quarterly,* the *Journal for Vocational Special Needs Education,* and the *Journal of Industrial Teacher Education.*

CYNTHIA ANN BOWMAN is an associate professor of literacy education at Ashland University in Ohio. She is an active member of the National Council of Teachers of English, the Conference on English Education, AERA, International Reading Association, and president-elect of the Ohio Council of Teachers of English Language Arts. She is coeditor of the English section of the online journal *Contemporary Issues in Technology and Teacher Education.* She has published numerous articles, book chapters, and texts, and her research interests include literacy, technology, reluctant learners, and disability.

CHRIS CRUTCHER is author of *Running Loose, Stotan! Chinese Handcuffs, Crazy Horse Electric Game, The Deep End, Staying Fat for Sarah Byrnes, Ironman,* and *Whale Talk.* His autobiography, *King of the Mild Frontier,* was released in April 2003, and a new novel is scheduled for publication in fall 2004. Crutcher's fast-paced fiction—heavily influenced by his work as a therapist and child protection advocate—is known for its expert balance of comedy and tragedy, as well as its unflinching honesty and authentic voice. He has received dozens of awards and honors.

PAMELA K. DELOACH is a special education teacher at Foster Elementary in Tampa, Florida, where she educates children with severe and profound mental disabilities. She has been a member of the Council for Exceptional Children (CEC) for 12 years and is currently codirector of the Educators with Disabilities Caucus. She has been awarded Teacher of the Year three times throughout her career.

ALLISON P. DICKEY graduated from the University of Central Florida with degrees in specific learning disabilities, varying exceptionalities, and curriculum and instruction with an emphasis in special education. During her teaching career in Orlando, she has worked with middle and high school students with disabilities and their families. She is currently an assistant professor of special education at Ashland University. Her research interests include exploration of the psychological/sociological dynamic of the disabled child in the family unit; the effect of the student's disability pertaining to socialization issues; educational learning and transition opportunities; students with disabilities and continuation of postsecondary education; and increasing effective communication between teachers, parents, students, and community support personnel at the secondary level.

PHYLLIS A. GORDON is associate professor and director of the master's program in counseling psychology and guidance services at Ball State University in Muncie, Indiana. Her research interests include attitude formation; group dynamics; family issues pertaining to chronic illness and severe, persistent mental illness; and multicultural and gender barriers to integration. Her teaching interests include vocational rehabilitation counseling; cultural sensitivity; and vocational psychology. She is a member of the American Psychological Association, American Counseling Association, National Council on Rehabilitation Education, and National Rehabilitation Association.

DAVID W. HARTMAN is a counseling psychologist in Salem, Virginia. He has written numerous articles and book chapters. He appeared on *60 Minutes* and often speaks on disability, family issues, and educational success.

PAUL T. JAEGER is senior research director and EBSCO Fellow at the Information Use Management and Policy Institute of Florida State University and is a doctoral student at Florida State University's School of Information Studies. He has earned a Juris Doctor and master's degrees in information studies and education. His publications have addressed issues of disability law and accessibility, information access, information policy, electronic government, education law, Constitutional law, and security and privacy. He is the coauthor, with Cynthia Ann Bowman, of *Disability Matters: Legal and Pedagogical Issues of Disability in Education* (Praeger, 2002).

TOM McNULTY is librarian for fine arts, as well as coordinator of services for people with disabilities, at New York University's Bobst Library. He holds an MA in Fine Arts (NYU), and an MLS from Queens College, City University of New York. McNulty is the coauthor of *Access to Information: Materials, Technologies and Services for People with Disabilities* (American Library Association, 1993) and the editor of and contributor to *Accessible Libraries on Campus* (Association of College and Research Libraries, 1999). The author of numerous articles on library service and disability, he is also the editor of the journal *Information Technology and Disabilities* (http://www.rit.edu/~easi/itd).

ANN NEVIN graduated from the University of Minnesota with a PhD in educational psychology. She has participated in the development of innovative teacher education programs since the 1970s, beginning with the Vermont Consulting Teacher Program. Dr. Nevin's wide-ranging research interests include cooperative learning methods to provide inclusive experiences for diverse learners, applications of reinforcement theory and applied behavior analysis, and developing self-determination skills within the K–12 curriculum for students with disabilities. She earned the 2001 Scholar of the Year award at Arizona State University West and professor emerita status in 2002.

MOLLY K. TSCHOPP is assistant professor of counseling psychology and guidance services at Ball State University in Muncie, Indiana. She has written several articles, including: "Career Counseling with People with Disabilities," "Addressing Issues of Sexuality with Adolescents with Disabilities," "Cognitive Assessment Issues with Older Persons," and "Career Development of Individuals with Psychiatric Disabilities: An Ecological Perspective of Barriers and Interventions." She is a member of the American Psychological Association, American Counseling Association, National Council on Rehabilitation Education, and National Rehabilitation Association.